# Kathy Kaehler's
## *Celebrity Workouts*

# How to Get a Hollywood Body in Just 30 Minutes a Day

# Kathy Kaehler's

## *Celebrity Workouts*

Broadway Books

New York

PRINTED IN THE UNITED STATES OF AMERICA

BROADWAY BOOKS and its logo, a letter B bisected on the diagonal, are trademarks of Random House, Inc.

*Book design by RLF Design*
*Photographs of Kathy Kaehler by Eric Asla*

ISBN 0-7394-4990-7

*To my best friend
and partner for life, Billy.*

# Contents

# Introduction

Have you ever looked at the sexy, sculpted celebrities who grace the pages of magazines like *People, Vogue,* and *InStyle* and thought, "If I had my own personal trainer, I'd be in great shape, too!"? With your time constraints and budget, some of you may secretly think that a Hollywood body is completely out of reach—only achievable if you have an arsenal of personal trainers, stylists, a membership to the toniest gym, and all the latest workout gear at your command. Well, guess again. Having worked with many of Hollywood's leading ladies, I know what it takes to get them looking so slim and toned—and believe it or not, it *is* attainable for women just like you and me. In this book, I'm excited to share all of my trade secrets with you. From here on in, whether you're an aspiring actress, a schoolteacher, or a stay-at-home mom, I will be your very own personal trainer, giving you all of the guidance and support you need to get fit, shed unwanted pounds, and feel like a million bucks.

Despite what you may think, you don't have to exercise for three hours a day, spend thousands of dollars on high-end workout equipment, or banish carbohydrates from your diet to get lean and fit, and feel as sexy in your clothes as any screen siren. My body-sculpting plan doesn't require a major time commitment, so it's manageable no matter how insanely busy you are. And it doesn't require expensive gear or machines. The truth is that getting in shape is a lot simpler than you may think. With this program, you'll be doing the same simple but effective exercises as Jennifer Aniston, Julia Roberts, and my other celebrity clients. My easy-to-follow routines have worked for them, and they can work for you, too. Likewise, this book provides nutrition advice that is 100 percent healthy and realistic—no flashy gimmicks with questionable promises—so you can lose excess weight safely and achieve lasting results.

By picking up this book, you've already taken an important first step toward changing your body—and your life—forever. If you want to look good for a special event, such as a wedding or college reunion, or get back in shape after having a baby or simply falling off the exercise wagon, this program will help you achieve your ideal figure. Whether you've never exercised before, you have trouble sticking with it, or are simply frustrated by lack of progress and results, you'll discover everything you need to know to turn over a new leaf and kick-start your motivation. Best of all, you'll learn how to make permanent lifestyle changes, so you'll never have to feel overweight or out of shape again.

When my fitness career began more than twenty years ago, I certainly didn't expect that many of my clients would end up being well-known TV and movie stars, supermodels, singers, and journalists, from Meg Ryan and Sarah Jessica Parker to Barbra Streisand and Maria Shriver. After all, I grew up in an average American family in an average suburban Michigan town. I'll admit that being part of the Hollywood scene can be fun. I've not only been lucky to work with some of the biggest names in the business, I occasionally get to go to film premieres and star-studded parties, too. But regardless of the glitz and glamour, what matters to me is teaching other people how to stay fit and healthy. I love giving them the knowledge and tools needed to look and feel their best.

Fortunately for me, I discovered the power of exercise at an early age. I began taking ballet, jazz, and tap dancing when I was nine years old, and continued through college. As I got older, I also played basketball and volleyball, and ran track. But while I've been active all my life, I've had my own struggles with weight. Between two pregnancies (during which I gained eighty and forty pounds, respectively) and an eating disorder in my late teens and early twenties, I've had my share of ups and downs. In our fast-paced, stressed-out, image-fixated, temptation-ridden society, I know firsthand how challenging it can be to get moving, eat healthy, and feel good about your body. However, I also know that it *is* possible to overcome bad habits, learn to enjoy working out, and dramatically improve the shape of your physique.

## My True Hollywood Story

People often ask me how I came to be a personal trainer to the stars. If you really want to know, it began with an introduction to actress Jane Fonda in the summer of 1987. I was working as a fitness instructor at a health club in Denver when my colleague and mentor, exercise physiologist Daniel Kosich, Ph.D., left to take a consulting job with Jane. Naturally, I was in awe. Jane is not only the star of some of my all-time-favorite movies (*On Golden Pond, Nine to Five,* and *The Morning After*), she's an exercise icon who revolutionized the fitness industry when she released Jane Fonda's Workout video in 1982 to instantaneous success. She followed it with a series of twenty-three other videos, thirteen audio recordings, and five books that sold a total of sixteen million copies.

In short, Jane was—and remains—my idol. I would have given anything to work with her. So I was absolutely thrilled when Daniel called me about six months later and said, "Jane is opening a spa and she's looking for someone to teach exercise classes. I've told her about you, and she wants to meet you." He explained that Jane had a ranch in the Santa Barbara Mountains that she wanted to turn into a retreat for people in the entertainment industry. Working with Jane Fonda would be nothing less than a dream come true for me. So I immediately packed up my bags and jumped on a plane bound for sunny California.

When I arrived at Los Angeles International Airport, I was full of anticipation. Daniel picked me up, and together we made the drive to Jane's Santa Barbara estate. After ninety minutes speeding down a crowded freeway and along twisty mountain roads, we pulled up to a huge arch with a sign that read LAUREL SPRINGS. That's when I really started to get nervous. My heart was racing, my palms were clammy, and I had trouble catching my breath. We pulled up to a cottage surrounded by rolling green lawns. There I was, sitting in the car, trying to take it all in and gain control of my breathing, when out she walked. *Jane Fonda.* I'd never been so excited in my life.

Jane stuck out her hand, and with a firm grip she shook my own sweaty one. (Naturally, she acted like she didn't notice the perspiration, which made me feel much more at ease.) We then went on a tour of the ranch.

As we walked around the grounds, I had to keep pinching my thigh to remind myself that this wasn't a dream.

Jane warned me that many of the spa's future clients, who would include famous actors and actresses, would probably be followers of exercise fads and veterans of crazy diets, like the cabbage soup and grapefruit diets. She made it clear that she wasn't a proponent of these fads. What's more, she wasn't looking for someone promising a "magic bullet" way to drop ten pounds in a weekend. She wanted someone who would teach clients how to make exercise a part of their lifestyle, so they weren't just slimming down to land a role. Jane truly had a passion for getting people up and moving. And it was contagious.

As Jane and I got to know each other, she told me that she had struggled with eating disorders when she was younger, and I opened up to her about some of the problems I'd had in high school and college. Because I hadn't liked the way I looked, I'd taken diet pills and become very ill with bulimia, which led to severe nutritional deficiencies. I had even been hospitalized a couple of times after having seizures caused by my terrible habits. I'd learned some hard lessons that eventually led me to develop a healthy and balanced approach to food and fitness, and I explained to Jane that I wanted to help other people learn to change their bodies and their lives through sensible eating and exercise. I was happy to discover that she and I were on the same page with our philosophies about safe weight loss and healthy lifestyles.

After my interview at Laurel Springs, I flew back to Denver and prayed that I'd get the job. I kept my fingers crossed for the entire flight home. When Daniel called me a few days later and offered it to me, I didn't even have to think about it. I just asked when I could start. I was elated—I couldn't believe that Jane Fonda had actually hired *me*, Kathy Kaehler!

Meeting Jane was a pivotal point for me both personally and professionally. Not only was I inspired by her passion for fitness, and her desire to share it with as many people as possible, but she helped shape my philosophies as a trainer. And as it turned out, the year I spent working at Laurel Springs literally opened the door for my Hollywood career.

## My Next Big Break

As a program director at Laurel Springs Spa, I worked closely with many celebrities, including actresses Melanie Griffith, Ally Sheedy, and Sharon Gless. I trained them one-on-one, took them hiking and mountain biking, and taught aerobics and toning classes. While I was excited to meet and get to know these talented women, I was surprised to discover that I didn't feel nervous around them. I'd been so starstruck when I first met Jane that, in comparison, everyone else seemed like a piece of cake, and I've rarely felt uneasy or intimidated around celebrities since. Take away the cameras and the make-up and the designer gowns, and they're just regular people, like the rest of us.

Unfortunately, the spa wasn't as successful as Jane had hoped it would be, and she was forced to close its doors a year later. Just as I was starting to panic about what to do next, I got a call from Melanie, who had just landed her now-famous role in the movie *Working Girl*. She wanted me to come to New York City to be her personal trainer during the filming. I jumped at the chance.

Melanie was my first "on-location movie star" gig, and I worked with her for two months during *Working Girl*. Seeing Melanie transform herself into the energetic Tess McGill—who stole Harrison Ford's heart and gave Sigourney Weaver a run for her money—was truly gratifying. When I watched her shine in that role, I felt like I'd played a part in some small way. It was a lot of fun, and Melanie and I became fast friends. We even went to the famous Limelight disco together once when we took a night off from working out.

But truth be told, life on the movie set wasn't as exciting or glamorous as I expected. The cast and crew spent a lot of time waiting around until it was their turn to shoot a scene. Sometimes Melanie had to be on set all day, from the wee hours of the morning until late at night. Some stars have a designated "workout trailer" with weights and cardio equipment, but Melanie didn't. So her only option was to exercise well before the crack of dawn, or at the very end of the day.

When my gig with Melanie was over I went on to Montecito, California, and decided to try building a business as a personal trainer. I commuted to Los Angeles every day so I could train Pamela Des Barres, bestselling author of *I'm with the Band* and *Take Another Little Piece of My Heart,* whom I had also met at Laurel Springs. Pamela then introduced me to the Zappas—Frank, Gail, Dweezil, Moon, Ahmet, and Diva—who became my clients, too. The Zappas were such an incredible, hilarious family. Even by today's standards, they'd make the Osbornes seem tame!

Soon those first few clients sparked a chain reaction. Through the Zappas, I met actresses Beverly D'Angelo and Brooke Shields. Then, through Pamela, I began training Julianne Phillips, who starred on *Sisters,* one of my all-time-favorite television shows, and actress Penelope Ann Miller, who became a longtime client and friend. In fact, it was Penelope who took me to a party for her movie *Other People's Money,* where I met my husband, Billy, who was there as a guest of an assistant to Danny DeVito. As a small-town girl from Rochester Hills, Michigan, I never imagined myself rubbing shoulders with the stars, much less meeting the love of my life through one of them.

Word of mouth in Hollywood spreads fast, and my personal training business really began to take off. Before long, my roster also included Claire Forlani, Justine Bateman, Candice Bergen, Michele Pfeiffer, and Jami Gertz. All of a sudden, I was booked seven days a week with clients such as Julia Roberts, Denise Richards, Lisa Kudrow, Jennifer Aniston, Rita Wilson, Barbra Streisand, Meg Ryan, Maria Shriver, Cindy Crawford, Claudia Schiffer, and Rob Lowe. The pages in my appointment book began to look like something out of *Variety* or Page Six in the *New York Post.*

Behind the scenes, even though we weren't married yet, Billy was actively trying to help me build my career. He helped me secure a deal to make my first exercise video, *The Kathy Kaehler Fitness System,* which included appearances by some of my famous clients. But I didn't want to stop there. I wanted to continue spreading my message and helping even more people discover the power of exercise. In a nutshell, I wanted to be more like Jane Fonda.

### "Hello, This Is Katie Couric . . ."

Growing up, I remember watching the *Today* show. My mother always had it on in the kitchen, and we ate breakfast while watching the show every morning. It almost felt like the hosts were a part of our family. After leaving the nest, I had continued this tradition, tuning in whenever possible. One morning about ten years ago, it occurred to me that the show could use a regular fitness segment. Television seemed like the perfect vehicle to educate millions of Americans on the benefits of exercise and help them get off their couches and start moving. If they couldn't make it to a gym or weren't sure where to begin, the *Today* show could deliver fitness advice and easy workouts right into their living rooms. And who better to show them how than me? So I sat down and wrote Katie Couric a heartfelt letter outlining my vision and expertise.

Much to my surprise, Katie actually read my letter and was interested enough to call me herself. I wasn't home at the time, so Billy answered the phone—of course, he thought it was a prank at first. But when Katie mentioned the letter that I had worked so hard on, he quickly realized that this wasn't a joke. He took a message and called me on my cell phone right away. I was ecstatic! I couldn't believe that Katie Couric had read my letter, much less taken the time to call.

I immediately called her back, and even though I was a nervous wreck, she instantly made me feel at ease. In real life, she's just as warm and funny as she appears on television. In my letter to her, I'd mentioned my plans to be in New York later in the month, and she invited me to visit the NBC studio while I was in town. I was completely blown away. After thanking her profusely, I hung up the phone, afraid that I would wake up to discover it had all been a dream.

A few weeks later, as Katie's guest at the studio, I was allowed into a special viewing room where I watched the *Today* show being filmed. Afterward, when I met with Katie in her office, she said, "Let's talk about how we can get you on the show." Needless to say, I was immensely flattered and excited that she was taking me under her wing and giving me so much of her time.

Later that day, Katie introduced me to Bryant Gumbel, who was Katie's cohost at the time, and to the show's executive producer, Jeffrey Zucker. To my delight, Jeff asked me to do a trial fitness segment. Everything seemed to be happening so fast. On the day we filmed my first segment live in Studio 1A in Rockefeller Plaza, I had serious butterflies in my stomach. I'd been in front of a camera once or twice before, but I was still very anxious. I knew that this was the opportunity of a lifetime, and I didn't want to blow it.

As it turned out, the segment went so smoothly and got such a great response from the show's producers that Katie called and asked me to appear on a regular basis. When I told Billy the news, I was so excited that I could hardly speak. Never in my wildest dreams had I imagined that something like this would happen to me. Almost immediately, the paperwork began and I had a signed contract.

That's when my life started to get *really* hectic! My training schedule was still booked solid, and now I was flying to New York twice a month to appear on the *Today* show. But to this day, the show gives me so much energy and motivation. You simply can't be around people like Katie, Matt, Al, and Ann and not be in high spirits. From the popular hosts to the camera crew, everyone is so friendly, down to earth, and enthusiastic about the work they're doing that it truly feels like a second home.

## Why I Wrote This Book

These days I still have a full workload, and then some. I fly to New York at least once a month to appear on the *Today* show. Then there are other work-related projects, like doing consulting work for Royal Caribbean

Cruises, appearing as a spokesperson for the Milk Board, the WalkMill™, and other organizations and products, and even doing special guest appearances on the soap opera *As the World Turns*. Last and certainly not least, I'm the mother of three young children: eight-year-old twins, Cooper and Payton, and four-year-old Walker.

Needless to say, I'm constantly running around, trying to fulfill my professional duties and, more important, to be a good mom and wife. But no matter what, I make time for exercise. Even if it's only for ten minutes, I'm committed to doing some sort of physical activity most days of the week. Even though I don't always feel like it, I do it because I *know* I'll feel better afterward. Whether I'm lifting weights, power walking, playing catch with my boys, or cleaning the house, exercise makes me feel so much better physically and mentally. It helps me stay grounded and gives me the energy that I need to keep up with my hectic life, a life that I love.

I know from experience how hard it can be to fit exercise into an overbooked schedule. Not only do *I* have a crazy calendar; so do most of my prominent clients. Designing effective workouts to fit chaotic lives has been one of my trademarks. And since I know that it isn't just Hollywood types that are booked 24/7, this book will outline my strategies for you.

I also know that, even with the red-carpet razzle-dazzle that's a part of everyday life in Los Angeles, fitness doesn't have to be complicated or cost a fortune. Whether I'm working with high-profile celebrities or regular people, I keep my routines as simple as possible. When I stick to the basics, I find my clients are more likely to stick with the program. With my plan, you don't have to join a gym or purchase a lot of expensive equipment. Instead, you'll be using ordinary household items, such as a deck of cards, masking tape, and a chair, which makes it easy to get started. I truly believe this is one of the reasons I've made a name for myself in Hollywood: My workouts are straightforward and can be performed in the privacy of your own home. And best of all, *they get results*.

Despite its catchy title and flashy packaging, this isn't a trendy, quick-fix fitness book. I'm not into the fads and gimmicks touted in magazines and hawked on television. Mostly because that's not real life. Physical fitness can't be achieved with a magic fat-burning pill or a highfalutin machine that you use for ten minutes a day. Like it or not, no matter who you are, it requires an ongoing commitment. My goal is to help you channel that inspiration and motivation we all feel when we see someone with a fabulous body, and develop an exercise habit that will last a lifetime.

If you haven't exercised in months or even years, the plan that follows is the perfect place to start. My weekly program includes a different workout for each day, so you won't get bored. You'll do cardio and strength routines to blast calories and increase strength and muscle tone. The result: total-body lifting, tightening, and toning, even in those "impossible" spots. Different levels of resistance will increase the benefit, whether you're using your own body weight only or using hand weights. I'll help you start at the level that's right for you and work your way up from there. I'll explain also how to make your days more active, so you can burn more calories and improve your muscle tone without even feeling like you're exercising.

Remember: Fitness isn't about having a perfect body, and even Hollywood knows this. In recent years, actresses like Catherine Zeta-Jones, Megan Mullally, and Drew Barrymore have proven that curves can be just as sexy as a tall and slender shape. It's about staying healthy, feeling good, and looking your best. Sure, we'd all like to look like the gorgeous starlets walking down the red carpet at the Oscars. But we also need to learn to accept our natural body types. Let's face it, I'm not and never will be 5'10" and 120 pounds, like some of today's supermodels. No matter what kind of exercises I do, I'll never have superlong, slim legs like Julia Roberts or slender hips like Claudia Schiffer. Instead I've learned to be happy with my body, especially when I'm in shape and feeling healthy. However, using Hollywood stars as fitness role models is terrific for the inspiration they give us to work out regularly and take care of our bodies. Keep in mind that they all work hard to maintain their shapes—and using their secrets, you can achieve and maintain your best shape, too.

Perhaps, like many people, you already spend a lot of time and energy thinking about your body and your weight. If so, it's already a priority in your mind. Now, let's make it a priority in your actions. Rather than complaining about how you look or the numbers on the scale, get busy! You can have the glow of a Hollywood diva, the energy of a teenager, and your best body ever. It's all up to you. So what are you waiting for? Let's get moving!

# Kathy Kaehler's
## Celebrity Workouts

# My Hollywood Fitness Secrets . . . Revealed!

**P**sssst . . . *Want me to let you in on a little Holly-* wood secret? The beautiful, sexy bodies that you see on television and the silver screen aren't simply the product of good genes. Not all of your favorite celebrities were born with impeccable figures, or have been slim and sculpted their entire lives. In fact, most of them have to work hard to stay so trim, toned, and youthful looking—just like you and me.

Though we tend to put them on pedestals, celebrities aren't superhuman. Some, particularly supermodels like Cindy Crawford and Claudia Schiffer, may have genetic advantages. But they still have to exercise and watch what they eat. And it isn't always easy! Like you and me, they have lazy days. They sometimes feel uncoordinated when trying a new workout. They get bored when they do the same exercises over and over. They have cravings for pizza, ice cream, and other fattening foods. They often want to do nothing more than collapse on the couch after a long, exhausting day on the set.

My celebrity clients may not have traditional nine-to-five jobs, but they certainly don't have all day to spend at the gym. Truth be told, none of the actresses or models that I train typically exercises for more than an hour at a time. These women are unbelievably busy! Whether they're working on a movie, a TV sitcom, a fashion show, or a photo shoot, their schedules tend to be very demanding. I'm talking ten- to twelve-hour days! On top of their chaotic careers, they have families, bills, grocery shopping, errands, and countless other responsibilities, just like everyone else. And most of them don't have a team of personal assistants to help them, either. Take Julia Roberts, for example. She doesn't even hire someone to clean her house. She washes her own dishes, scrubs her own bathroom, and mops her own kitchen floor.

Celebrities are constantly subjected to the scrutiny of the camera, whether they're on a film set, walking the red carpet, or running from the paparazzi. If you can imagine having your body magnified on screen, or photos of yourself plastered all over the tabloids, then you may understand the kind of motivation that they have to look good. Sadly, for some, the pressure can be overwhelming. In recent years a number of them, such as Paula Abdul and Carré Otis, have started coming forward and sharing their struggles to remain so unnaturally thin. To keep the pounds off, some have resorted to unhealthy, even potentially life-threatening tactics, such as excessive exercise, vomiting, drug and alcohol abuse, cigarette smoking, and harsh diuretics. Others have gone under the plastic surgeon's knife for procedures like liposuction and tummy tucks.

Fortunately, Hollywood has finally woken up to the realization that super-thin is super-unattractive and super-unhealthy. A decade or so ago in the entertainment industry, "skinny Minnie" wasn't skinny enough. Size Zero was the norm in Los Angeles. But in just the last few years, the "ideal" body shape has started to change. The waif look is out. Fit and toned is in! What's sexy is looking strong, lean, and healthy. Many of our favorite stars—including Catherine Zeta-Jones and Jennifer Lopez—are now embracing their curves. And we all know that's what men really love!

I know all about the dangers of trying to be skinny. Although I'd never worried about my weight as a kid, I became unhappy with my appearance in high school. I wasn't overweight; I had a sturdy, athletic frame. But I didn't think I was thin enough. During my senior year, I started taking over-the-counter diet pills to lose weight. This insane habit continued into my college years, when I also battled bulimia. On a typical morning I would swallow a diet pill, then go without food until I was absolutely starving. After bingeing to satisfy my hunger, I'd run to the ladies' room to vomit. At one point I was taking up to five diet pills a day.

One afternoon during my sophomore year, it all started to unravel. As I was walking out of my dorm room, I suffered a grand-mal seizure. I woke up on the sidewalk with a paramedic kneeling beside me. Later, in the hospital, I lied to my doctors, telling them the seizure must have been caused by stress and lack of sleep. They believed me, and I was released from the hospital. But even this scary experience wasn't enough to make me quit. I continued in the vicious binge-purge-pill cycle for another year, until I finally had another seizure. Realizing that I would die if I didn't change my behavior, I vowed to stop taking diet pills and stop throwing up.

With every bit of self-discipline I had, I took control of my life. I educated myself about healthy eating and started giving my body the nutrients that it so badly needed. I have never taken diet pills or vomited since. My all-around good habits lasted about six years, up until the time that I moved to Los Angeles. At that point, my career was going full throttle, and I had a full schedule training clients and teaching aerobics classes. But I was overexercising and not eating enough. At the same time, I was dating a famous actor who liked to stay up all night and sleep all day. I was partying too much and only getting a few hours of shut-eye each night. During the day, I was drinking tons of coffee just to keep myself going.

Throughout all of this, my body was suffering. I felt tired and worn out. I realized that I wasn't living healthfully, and as someone whose career was based on promoting health and fitness, I felt like a total hypocrite. Then, in 1990, it caught up with me. I suffered a third seizure while hiking with a client. At the hospital, my doctor threatened to put me on antiseizure medication, which meant my driver's license would be taken away. Since my livelihood depended on driving to see my clients, I promised him that I would change my habits the moment that I walked out the door. And I did. After that day, I completely overhauled my lifestyle. I started eating right and sleeping eight hours a night. I also pledged to give up caffeine for good. Thankfully, I've been in excellent health ever since.

Over the years, I've learned a tremendous amount, both personally and professionally, about how to stay fit, healthy, and looking good. Most of my career has been spent sharing this know-how with a Who's Who of the entertainment industry. Now, it's time for me to teach *you*. In this chapter, you'll find out all about my personal approach to fitness. I'll outline easy ways for you to squeeze more activity into your hectic days, and provide easy-to-follow eating guidelines. I'll also discuss the basic principles of weight loss, and tell you why a change in your attitude could be the secret to your success.

But the most important thing to remember is: No matter how much you want to look a certain way, no matter how badly you want to get into those slim-fitting jeans, and no matter how many daydreams you may have about looking like the fabulous women who populate our favorite films and television shows, your health is so much more important. Trust me, I say this to all my clients. In this book, we're going to work hard to get your body into amazing shape. But we're also going to respect it and embrace it—it's the only one you've got.

## The Exercise Equation

No matter who you are, in order to stay young and healthy, you need to move your body. It's as simple as that. Almost every system in your body, from your cardiovascular system to your muscular and skeletal systems, benefits from regular physical activity. By staying active you can reduce your risk of numerous health problems, including heart disease, high blood pressure, many cancers, diabetes, and osteoporosis. Exercise helps strengthen your immune system, so you can fend off many of these life-threatening diseases as well as ailments as basic as the common cold.

As many of you know, regular exercise is also essential for staving off excess pounds. Despite the many fad diets currently making headlines, research consistently shows that a combination of exercise and a healthy diet is the best way to lose weight and keep it off. By getting up and moving, you can burn calories that would otherwise be stored as fat. When you build muscle, you also speed up your metabolism, so your body burns more calories throughout the day, whether you're pushing a cart through the supermarket or sitting around watching TV.

But the benefits don't end there! Exercise can also have a powerful effect on your state of mind. During physical activity, your brain releases neurotransmitters called endorphins that can help elevate your mood and reduce feelings of stress and anxiety. Studies show that regular exercise can be as effective as antidepressants in alleviating mild to moderate depression. When you're feeling overworked and exhausted, exercise can help restore your energy, optimism, clarity, and creativity. After a good work-out, you'll be more productive and make better decisions. You'll also be much less likely to fly off the handle.

It follows, therefore, that exercise can have a huge impact on what you're able to achieve in life. When you're better able to handle physiolog-ical and emotional stress, you feel more in control of your life. You sleep better. You feel better about yourself. You have more confidence, whether you're making a presentation at work or slipping into your favorite dress—or, in the case of my famous clients, accepting an Academy Award or shooting a steamy bedroom scene.

When a client comes to me wanting to get in shape for a movie role, a TV appearance, or a fashion show, I always remind them that exercise shouldn't be a temporary fix. The same goes for those of you who picked up this book determined to lose weight or firm up for a special occasion—a wedding, a reunion, or a trip to a tropical locale for spring break. There's nothing more motivating than knowing you're going to be bumping into your ex or wearing a swimsuit in public! But if you want lasting results, you need to make fitness a permanent part of your life.

Fitness isn't just a goal—it's a lifestyle that will allow you to look and feel your best, and in turn, to live your best life. It isn't a superficial luxury; it's a necessity for health and well-being. The celebrities in this book look so stunning because they have made fitness a regular part of their routine. They may not always enjoy it, but they've committed to it, and *that*—com-bined with a knockout exercise regimen—is what gets them superstar re-sults. In this book, we'll do the same for you. You may not love working out, but if you stick with it, I promise that you'll love what it does for your body! And, as you get stronger, you may even find yourself craving every opportunity to get up and move.

## The Triangle of Fitness

Physical fitness has three integral parts: cardiovascular fitness, strength, and flexibility. All three components are vital for a healthy, balanced body—and should be the basis of any solid fitness plan.

Cardiovascular exercise works one of your most important muscles—your heart—along with your lungs. If you do cardio workouts regularly, your heart won't have to work as hard to pump blood through your body, and your lungs will deliver oxygen with less effort. This translates into more endurance and staying power, whether you're running after your kids or competing in a bike race. Because cardio burns a lot of calories, it's also an important tool for losing weight.

The second component, strength training, helps work important muscles in other areas of your body—your legs, buttocks, hips, arms, shoulders, chest, back, and abs. As we get older, our muscles and bones get weaker, especially if we don't eat right or exercise enough. Strength exercises can help prevent or even reverse these losses, reducing your risk of osteoporosis. Furthermore, if your muscles are strong, you're less likely to suffer back pain and other debilitating injuries. You also have the strength

## Metabolism 101

Your own body's composition is the primary factor determining your resting metabolic rate (RMR)—that is, the number of calories your body burns at rest. The more totally fat-free mass you have (including lean muscle, bones, and organs), the higher your RMR will be. After age thirty, the average woman's RMR decreases at a rate of 2 to 3 percent per decade, mainly due to inactivity and muscle loss. Fortunately, some of that loss can be prevented or even reversed with regular exercise, especially strength training.

Strength training helps you build and preserve lean muscle, which is the only way to permanently raise your RMR. Aerobic exercise also provides a temporary metabolic boost, although it doesn't have a lasting effect. A vigorous cardio workout that really raises your heart rate can elevate your metabolism by up to 20 percent. Afterward, your metabolism will slowly return to normal over the course of a few hours—but you'll continue burning calories in the meantime.

Keep in mind that whenever you lose weight, your RMR will actually slow down since you have less body mass to support. As a result, you'll need fewer calories to sustain your vital bodily functions. To continue dropping pounds, you'll need to eat a little less, increase the intensity of your workouts, or add more activity to your day. Otherwise you'll eventually hit a weight-loss plateau.

to pursue your next adventure, whether it's a hike through a national park or a long day at Disneyland.

Many women think that cardiovascular exercise, such as jogging or walking on a treadmill, is the best and only way to trim down. That's just plain wrong. In fact, strength training is the secret weapon of many of Hollywood's hottest female stars. It allows you to develop specific muscles for that sexy, sculpted look we all admire. When you build muscle, you not only look more defined, your metabolism gets a boost, so you burn more calories all day long. Muscle weighs more than fat, but it takes up less space—so even if the numbers on the scale don't change, your clothes will get looser, and your body will begin to look firmer and more taut.

The last piece of the triangle is flexibility. Our muscles are like rubber bands—they are incredibly resilient. But the less you use them, the tighter they get. Flexibility is crucial for preventing injuries and staying mobile. By stretching regularly you can keep your muscles limber, increase your range of motion, improve your balance, and enhance your posture. What's more, research suggests that stretching immediately after your strength-training workouts can help you build more muscle for an even bigger metabolic boost.

## How Much Is Enough?

And now for the million-dollar question: How much exercise do you have to do to get all of the benefits and achieve your best body? For weight control and optimum health, experts recommend at least 30 to 60 minutes of moderate exercise most days of the week. Thirty minutes a day can help you achieve important health benefits, and is a good starting goal if you're currently sedentary. As you get in better shape, you'll want to aim for closer to an hour, and/or work on increasing the intensity of your workouts, for even more benefits and calories burned.

This may sound overwhelming to those of you who haven't been exercising regularly. But don't get discouraged! With my program you'll start slowly, and gradually work on building strength. You can also do the workouts at your own pace. If time is an issue for you, and you're worried that you won't fit it all in, remember that the benefits of exercise are cumulative.

In other words, you don't have to do your 30 to 60 minutes all at once. Instead, you can do some in the morning, some at lunch, and some in the late afternoon. (You'll find more details on this type of scheduling in Chapter 2.)

When it comes to fitness, some activity is always better than none. But too much exercise isn't a good thing, either. I found this out the hard way. At the start of my career in Hollywood, I was working out way too much—even for a personal trainer! On a typical weekday, I'd train five or six clients in a row in the morning, then teach two back-to-back step aerobics classes at night. Even though I thought I was in great shape, I soon discovered that overexercising can lead to injury and burnout. I was fatigued and frequently in pain from one overuse injury or another.

Your exercise sessions should invigorate you, not wipe you out. So it's important to find a happy medium. These days, I take a much more moderate approach. And to tell you the truth, I feel much healthier, and my body looks about the same. Fortunately, this message has also caught on in Hollywood, and I no longer see as much of the exercise mania that gripped the industry a few years ago.

### Stealth Fitness

As little as a century ago, physical activity was necessary for survival. Just think how much energy it took to wash clothes, knead bread, churn butter, milk cows, chop wood, and walk miles to the nearest store. Today our lives are much easier. We have automobiles to transport us. We use washing machines and dryers. We take elevators, escalators, and moving walkways instead of walking or climbing stairs. We don't even have to get up to change the TV channel. I suppose if we wanted to, we'd barely have to move at all.

All of these modern conveniences can be a blessing, but they can also be a curse. Because of them, we have to make a major effort to work physical activity into our busy lives. Although a formal exercise program, such as the one in this book, is the most effective way to burn calories and improve your fitness level, you can also do wonders by simply adding more movement to your daily life. I call this stealth fitness, and research shows that these little bits of activity can help you improve your health, boost your energy, and fend off excess pounds.

For me, it's become a daily game—how many extra calories can I burn by moving more? There are countless opportunities to move—it's up to you to find them. For example, you can park your car in the back row of the parking lot. Do laps around the airport while you're waiting for a flight. Take stairs instead of an elevator or escalator whenever possible. Do biceps curls as you wait in line at the bank. Do jumping jacks while waiting for a pot of water to boil. Do squats as you brush your teeth. Get up and change the TV channel rather than use the remote. Rake your yard. Weed your garden. Wash your car. Go for a bike ride or play kickball with your children. If you're planning an evening out, don't resort to the traditional dinner and a movie. Try something active—dancing, bowling, or even mini-golf. Be creative!

Another way to sneak more exercise into your life is by taking active vacations. At least once or twice a year, I plan a fitness getaway with my family. Last spring, for instance, we sailed around Cuba on a Royal Caribbean Cruise that offered a wide range of athletic activities, from water skiing and kayaking to in-line skating to rock climbing. I'm not the kind of person who likes sitting around, so I loved every second of it. It gave us an opportunity to explore a new place while trying different activities. Best of all, I returned home feeling fit and invigorated! You can plan your own active adventure, or sign up for a group trip. From hiking to biking to multi-sport to yoga, there are some amazing options for different interests, fitness levels, and budgets.

## Healthy Eating

*Carbs are good. Carbs are bad. Eat red meat. Don't eat red meat. Don't use butter, but don't use margarine either!* No question—the subject of nutrition can be confusing. We get conflicting messages all the time. How are we supposed to know what to put in our mouths? And even if we have good intentions, we are surrounded by unhealthy food choices and gargantuan portions. Is it any wonder that so many Americans are struggling to lose weight?

Chances are some of you are frustrated because you've tried every diet under the sun with no success. Maybe you love to eat and weren't able to give up your favorite foods. Or maybe you simply couldn't live on cottage cheese and celery sticks. Well, you'll be happy to know that you don't have to deprive yourself or cut out entire food groups in order to slim down. Healthy eating doesn't have to be strict or complicated, and it definitely shouldn't mean starving yourself.

### Weighty Issues

Not long ago, I was reading John Grisham's book *The Partner.* In the book, the main character loses a lot of weight to change his appearance. When a judge asks him how he did it, he replies: "Losing weight is between the ears. Make up your mind and it's easy!" Now that's what I call a good piece of fiction!

Obviously, if slimming down were so easy, millions of Americans wouldn't be overweight. I'm the first to admit that shedding excess pounds, even just five or ten, can be difficult and frustrating. I gained eighty pounds during my first pregnancy, and I had to work hard to get rid of it. It took more than a year for me to get back to my prepregnancy weight. But the good news is, weight loss is possible for almost everyone. You can drop those excess pounds as long as you're willing to make long-term lifestyle changes and take it slowly.

Everywhere we go, we see promises of new systems and products to help us drop pounds, and crazy claims as to what really works. Many of these weight-loss products advertise fast and dramatic results—"Lose ten pounds in forty-eight hours!"—and one method is always better than the next. By some estimates, it's a $50-billion-a-year business. But don't buy into it unless you want to lose mostly water weight, and you enjoy that feeling of failure as the pounds creep back on.

There is no secret formula for weight loss. Instead, it's a simple numbers game. Here's how it works: One pound of body fat equals 3,500 calories. So to lose one pound of body fat a week, you need to create a weekly deficit of 3,500 calories, or 500 calories per day. Sounds simple, right? However, to avoid a major metabolic drop, you must do it through a combination of exercise and healthy eating. For example, if you consume 200 fewer calories each day, you'll have a weekly deficit of 1,400 calories. Burn an extra 2,100 calories per week, or 300 per day, through exercise, and you'll have met your goal.

For safe, lasting weight loss, you should aim to lose no more than one or two pounds a week. Any more than that is unrealistic, and if any program offers quicker results, you should think twice. Also, to keep your metabolism from nosediving, you shouldn't eat fewer than 1,200 calories a day. Remember, months and years of weight gain cannot be reversed in a matter of days! It will take some time to lose those extra pounds. Losing weight may be one of the hardest challenges that you ever face, but the effort will be worth it!

### The Diet Trap

Ironically, one of the biggest weight-loss mistakes that women make is not eating enough. Although it may seem counterintuitive, you need to eat in order to shed pounds permanently. Why? When you severely restrict calories, your metabolism slows down to conserve energy—it's your body's way of protecting itself from starvation. The more calories you cut, the lower your RMR drops. While you may lose weight at first, most of it is from water loss and the deterioration of muscle tissue, not from less fat. As soon as you return to your regular eating habits, you're apt to gain back the weight you lost, and possibly more, because you're no longer burning calories as efficiently.

Some of you may be wondering about the low-carbohydrate diets—including Atkins, South Beach, and The Zone—that are all the rage in Hollywood right now. The truth is that the jury is still out as to whether low-carb diets are any more effective than traditional low-fat diets over time. While these plans can produce quick weight loss, it happens because you're limiting calories, not because of some magic nutritional formula. And that's if you can stay on one! Some people may be able to live without bread, pasta, and cereal, but I know I can't. Often, as soon as you reintroduce carbohydrates into your diet, the pounds reappear.

Furthermore, no long-term studies have been done to determine the potential health risks of these high-fat, high-protein diets. In the past, research has shown that diets high in saturated fat can put you at risk for heart disease. What's more, experts fear that a diet very high in animal protein could increase your risk of osteoporosis and kidney problems. In addition, if you severely limit carbohydrates, you're apt to miss out on important vitamins, minerals, and fiber that you can't get from a supplement. This could result in nutritional deficiencies, along with lethargy, digestive problems, and bad breath.

Some popular diets also tell you to avoid "high-glycemic index" foods—that is, foods that are absorbed quickly into your bloodstream, potentially causing your blood sugar to spike and increasing fat storage. On these diets' "Do Not Eat" list are bananas, watermelon, sweet potatoes, corn, and carrots. Given the health benefits of these nutrient-packed foods, any diet book that tells you to stop eating them should be questioned. Have you ever seen anyone get fat from eating watermelon and carrots? I don't think so! While it may be best to practice moderation, I wouldn't recommend dropping these healthy foods altogether. Instead, try consuming them in conjunction with a small amount of fat (for example, olive oil, fish oil, or low-fat dairy), which will slow the absorption of carbohydrates into your bloodstream. For example, eat your sweet potato with grilled tuna, watermelon with light vanilla yogurt, or sliced banana on whole grain cereal topped with skim milk.

### Understanding the Basics

It sounds obvious, but it's worth repeating here: Your body needs food in order to function properly. In our efforts to lose weight, we often ignore this most basic fact. So think of your body as a car. Without fuel, your car won't run. Use the wrong type of fuel, and you'll do serious damage to the car's engine. The same is true for the human body. If you don't eat right, you won't have the nutrients and energy you need to stay healthy and active.

By making smart food choices, you can fuel your body, stay lean and trim, and look and feel your best. When you eat well, it shows. Good health radiates outward through glowing skin and shiny hair. If you eat poorly, you'll soon see the damage you're causing: a poor complexion, dull hair, brittle nails, a lack of energy, and excess pounds.

Everything we eat is made up of various combinations of three basic macronutrients: carbohydrates, protein, and fat. All three macronutrients are necessary for a healthy body. Without a balance of carbohydrates (about 50 to 55 percent of total daily calories), protein (about 20 to 25 percent of total daily calories), and fat (about 20 to 25 percent of total daily calories), your body won't have all the building blocks it needs to function properly and keep you feeling healthy and energized.

Carbohydrates are your body's primary source of energy—they're the main fuel used by your brain, nervous system, and muscles. The carbohydrate family consists of the complex starches found in whole grains and breads, legumes, and beans, as well as the simple sugars found in fresh fruits, vegetables, and dairy products. Aside from supplying vitamins, minerals, and protein, these wholesome foods can be vital sources of dietary fiber, which makes you feel full and could protect you from heart disease and cancer. The carbohydrate category also includes the refined sugars (such as table sugar and high-fructose corn syrup) found in candy, cookies, donuts, and soda, which may give you a quick-fix sugar rush but won't nourish your body or provide sustained energy. Rule of thumb: When including carbs in your diet, always go for the natural, nutritious kind.

Protein is your body's chief building material. It's an essential component of all of your muscles, bones, skin, blood, organs, and glands. Your body needs it to grow and repair tissues, and to transport nutrients in and out of cells. Since dietary protein takes longer to digest than carbohydrates, it can help curb hunger. But you shouldn't go overboard: Excess protein could put a strain on your kidneys and may cause calcium to be excreted from your body. To keep your fat intake in check, you should stick to lean animal sources, such as poultry, fish, shellfish, egg whites, and non- or low-fat dairy products. You can also get protein from dried peas and beans, soy, seeds, and nuts.

Despite its bad rap, fat is also vital for energy, satiety, and overall good health. It's used to insulate your body tissues and transport fat-soluble vitamins through your blood, and also helps bring out the flavor in food. Fat is digested more slowly than either protein or carbohydrates, so it keeps you feeling satisfied longer. There are three types: unsaturated, saturated, and trans fats. Unsaturated fats, found in vegetable oils, nuts, avocados, and olives, are actually good for you and have been shown to lower cholesterol levels. On the other hand, saturated fats (which come from animal sources including meat, poultry, and dairy products such as cream, whole milk, butter, and shortening) and trans fats (found in fried foods, margarine, and processed snack foods made from hydrogenated vegetable oils) are the ones that raise cholesterol and put your heart at risk. *All* fats are high in calories, so it's important to use moderation.

### 8 Simple Rules for Healthy Eating

I don't believe in complicated or restrictive eating plans. In my book, there are no such things as "good" and "bad" foods. If you're going to stick with a healthy eating program, you need to keep it simple. That's why my food philosophy is based on the principles of balance, variety, moderation, and commonsense.

On the following pages, I've outlined my simple rules for healthy eating. While I urge you to make these dietary modifications, don't try to incorporate them all at once. If you attempt a complete overhaul on the first day, you're apt to feel overwhelmed. Instead, strive to make one or two small changes each week. Before you know it, you'll be eating better, feeling better, and losing weight without feel deprived or starved.

1. **Avoid processed foods.** As much as possible, go for fresh, wholesome foods that are in their natural state and have had minimal processing. Try to limit your intake of highly refined foods, which are typically sold in bags, boxes, and cans, and contain chemicals and other man-made ingredients. Also, beware of high-fructose corn syrup—commonly found in soft drinks, fruit drinks, and baked goods—which has been linked to weight gain and diabetes. By following this simple rule, you'll include more whole

grains and foods from the fruit and plant world, which are naturally nutritious and low in calories.

2. **Go for color.**  Choose lots of colorful fruits and vegetables, such as spinach, broccoli, red bell peppers, cantaloupe, sweet potatoes, oranges, blueberries, and kiwis. These vibrant choices are typically packed with vitamins and antioxidants. Go crazy and create a rainbow on your plate!

3. **Graze.**  Instead of the traditional three square meals a day, break your daily calories into several small meals and snacks (about 200 to 400 calories each), spread throughout the day. The goal is to never let yourself get too hungry or too full. By continuing to fuel your body throughout the day, you'll keep your metabolism elevated and prevent the dips in blood sugar that cause overeating. You'll also maintain a steady flow of energy for all of your activities.

4. **Don't skip meals.**  When we skip meals, we skip nutrition. In the past, you may have been thinking that you're saving calories. But as I said earlier, when you deprive yourself of food, your metabolic rate drops, so you actually burn fewer calories. Plus, if you don't eat, you'll find yourself starving a few hours later. The result will likely be bingeing on unhealthy food.

5. **Choose healthy fats.**  Fat can, and should, be part of a healthy diet. The trick is to limit your intake and consume the right type. Opt for unsaturated fats, like vegetable oils, nuts, and avocados, which typically come from plant sources. Limit foods high in saturated fats, such as fatty steaks and dairy products, which usually come from animal sources (two exceptions: coconut and palm oils). And steer clear of trans fats, which are derived from hydrogenated vegetable oils and are found in fried foods, margarine, and packaged snack foods like crackers.

6. **Fill up with fiber.**  Whole grains, fresh fruits, veggies, beans, and other fiber-rich foods not only make you feel full, they help whisk

food through your digestive tract, so fewer calories are absorbed. Studies also suggest that eating foods rich in soluble fiber can reduce your risk of heart disease and colon cancer. So not only are you satisfying those hunger pangs, you're doing something really good for your body. Oatmeal, grainy breads, broccoli, pears, berries, and lentils are all excellent sources of fiber.

7. **Watch your portion sizes.** We live in the land of supersize, and such incredibly large portions can wreak havoc on your waistline. So be careful. Read labels. Get out your measuring cups. Relearn how much cereal to put in a bowl and the correct serving size for a piece of chicken (the size of your computer mouse). Train yourself to order smaller portions. Learn to ask for a doggie bag. In restaurants, you can even ask for appetizer sizes, which are typically a standard portion size. And remember, you don't have to clean your plate!

8. **Limit caloric beverages.** Ever notice how quickly a drink goes down, especially when you're thirsty? If it's a sweetened cola,

## Water World

Just the other day—a typical Los Angeles scorcher—actress Penelope Ann Miller taught me a good way to drink and drive. Yes, you heard me right. She told me to keep a case of bottled water in the trunk of my car. This way, she told me, I wouldn't be tempted to grab a caffeinated soda or other beverage that is dehydrating or contains a lot of added sugars. Now, if I stop at a drive-through, I simply ask for a cup of ice. I've also found that it's easy to stash a cooler of ice in the trunk.

The benefits of water are almost endless. Water makes up about 60 percent of the average person's body, it aids in digestion, blood production, and breathing, and helps solid waste move through your intestines. Water lubricates your joints and helps regulate your body temperature, so it's especially important if you're exercising regularly. To top it off, it serves as a natural appetite suppressant. Aim for at least eight to ten glasses a day. I like keeping a bottle handy at all times and sipping frequently. If you get bored with plain water, try sparkling water or seltzer with flavored essence, a slice of fresh lime, or a splash of cranberry juice. Cheers!

lemonade, or iced tea, you may be chugging down more calories than you'd like to imagine—all without any real nutritional benefit. These beverages, along with specialty coffee drinks, can really sabotage a weight-loss plan. Instead of sipping empty calories, reach for water or a drink that delivers needed nutrients, such as green tea, skim milk, or fresh-squeezed juice diluted with water. I also recommend cutting back on caffeinated beverages. Caffeine robs your body of water and leaches calcium from your bones. Alcoholic drinks are also dehydrating and high in calories. So if you choose to imbibe, keep it to no more than one a day.

Now that I've shared my simple rules, I'm going to come clean. I love sweets and junk food, just like everyone else. So I've adopted what I call the 90/10 rule. Ninety percent of the time, I eat really well. I consume lots of fresh fruits, vegetables, whole grains, and lean protein. I go for complex carbohydrates, limit simple carbs, and watch my fat intake. And I always drink plenty of water. The other 10 percent of the time, I eat whatever I want, whether it's a slice of cheesy pizza, a chocolate chip cookie, or a Diet Coke. As long as you stick to my simple 90/10 guideline, you're doing great!

### Good Nutrition on the Go

If your idea of fixing dinner is making a reservation, you're not alone. Many of us are so busy all day long that we don't have time to stop at the supermarket, look up recipes, and spend an hour preparing a healthy meal. For others, eating out is social and relaxing. In the coming weeks, as you work on adopting a healthier lifestyle, start making the effort to prepare more meals at home—it's the best way to keep tabs on fat and calories, and boost your intake of fresh fruit and veggies. Every Sunday I try to plan all of my week's meals and do my grocery shopping, so my refrigerator is stocked with nutritious food. Of course, I still find myself grabbing a bite out every now and then. The good news is, it's almost always possible to find healthy eating options. The following survival tips will help you avoid poor food choices and unnecessary calories no matter where you go.

## Eating Healthy, Hollywood Style

Hollywood's leading ladies have a helping hand when it comes to eating well. Caterers are on the set to provide nutritious food while the cameras are rolling. Off the set, many of these same stars hire personal chefs to help them cook up body-conscious meals, or dine at restaurants that cater to healthy appetites. Unfortunately, the rest of us are on our own. That's why I've asked four top celebrity chefs—Carrie Wiatt, Hollis Wilder, Jamie Oliver (formerly known as the Naked Chef), and Wolfgang Puck—to share some of their favorite recipes to help you get started. Carrie, a nutritionist and author of the book *Portion Savvy,* has worked with a long list of Hollywood A-listers, including Sela Ward, Salma Hayek, Alfre Woodard, and Neve Campbell. A private chef for ten years, Hollis, who happens to be a regular at my Hidden Hills fitness classes, has worked on the sets of *Will & Grace, Good Morning Miami,* and *Boston Common.* Jamie Oliver, owner of Fifteen Restaurant in London, has his own television show, *Oliver's Twist,* on The Food Network and has authored three bestselling cookbooks. And of course everyone knows Wolfgang, a culinary powerhouse who co-owns several of the hottest eateries in Los Angeles, is author of five cookbooks, has his own line of cookware, and has starred in two shows (*Wolfgang Puck* and *Wolfgang Puck's Cooking Class*) on The Food Network. You'll find their recipes scattered throughout this book, along with a few of my own favorites. They're a perfect complement to the workouts ahead, and will give you some great ideas for the kinds of meals that can help you achieve your weight-loss goals. Bon appétit!

### Restaurants

When ordering, go for simple meals, such as fish or poultry with rice and veggies, instead of multiple-ingredient dishes like lasagna and casseroles. To keep fat and calories in check, always opt for grilled, broiled, or roasted meats and vegetables, rather than fried. Request sauces and salad dressings on the side. And ask the kitchen to "hold" fattening side dishes, such as mashed potatoes, French fries, or greasy potato chips. Remember: *You* are in the driver's seat at a restaurant. Most chefs will prepare food any way it's requested. So if you can't find a suitable option on the menu, don't hesitate to ask. If you're embarrassed, tell a little white lie (for example, "I'm lactose intolerant, so can you use olive oil instead of butter?"). Inquire about portion sizes before placing your order. If portions tend to be large, order off the appetizer menu, or ask your server to put half in a doggie bag before you're served. And take a pass on the bread basket or tortilla chips at your favorite Mexican restaurant.

### Fast-Food Joints

When you're on the road or in a rush, the drive-through is sometimes your only option. Fortunately, more and more fast-food restaurants are now offering healthier alternatives. McDonald's, for example, recently introduced the Go Active! Happy Meal, which includes a salad, bottled water, and a pedometer. Another great option is the Chicken McGrill sandwich. Burger King has the Savory Mustard Fire-Grilled Chicken Baguette. Subway offers several salads with light dressings. Pizza Hut now has thin-crust pizzas—just be sure to skip the pepperoni and extra cheese. Taco Bell has the "Fresco Style" menu. Even KFC has skinless chicken options. As a general rule, order small or regular sizes and avoid anything labeled Double, Deluxe, Super, Extra, Combo, or Jumbo. If you're ordering a sandwich, hold the mayonnaise, special sauce, cheese, and other fatty add-ons. If you're having a salad, go light on the dressing. And of course, avoid anything deep-fried.

### Movie Theaters

Movie-theater snack bars can spell dietary disaster if you aren't careful. The best idea, of course, is to eat before you get to the theater or bring a healthy snack with you, so you aren't tempted to fill up on junk. If you need a nibble, pick the smallest-size popcorn (even if it's the kiddie size) and skip the butter. If your theater sells candy by the pound, grab a bag and take a few fat-free Gummy Bears or Hot Tamales. If you're dying for chocolate, try a small candy bar or Rolos, which are individually wrapped. Many theaters now offer bottled water—always the best beverage choice.

### Parties

If you arrive at a party famished, you're almost guaranteed to overeat. So have a nutritious bite before heading out. Try a small meal or snack containing fiber, protein, and healthy fat, such as peanut butter on half an apple, sliced turkey on half a whole grain bagel, a cup of low-sodium chicken soup, low-fat cheese on whole wheat crackers, or edamame. This should prevent you from downing a lot of salty, fatty appetizers or attacking the buffet table. It will also help keep you from getting tipsy from one glass of wine, which can soften your resolve to eat healthy!

### Preventing Pig-outs

I've already explained how eating smaller, more frequent meals and consuming fiber-rich foods can help you feel more satisfied and keep hunger at bay. But for many of us overeating is a function of our mood more than of our need for nourishment. Stress, boredom, anger, and loneliness are common emotional triggers that cause us to overindulge. To make matters worse, temptations are everywhere, making it all too easy to dive into a chocolate cake or scarf down an entire box of cookies. What to do? Follow these strategies:

- **Think twice.** Ask yourself a few questions before downing whatever rich treat is in front of you. Are you really hungry? Or are you eating out of frustration, anger, annoyance, or loneliness? Identifying the cause of your cravings will help you control impulse eating. It may also give you a better understanding of feelings that may have sabotaged earlier weight-loss efforts.

## Boning Up on Calcium

*Drink your milk!* How many times did we hear that growing up? Turns out that our parents were right! The calcium found in milk and other dairy products helps fortify our bones. Getting enough calcium is not only imperative when you're growing, but also as you grow older. After the age of thirty-five, our bones start losing their density, especially during and after menopause. By consuming at least 1,000 to 1,300 milligrams of calcium a day, we can slow down bone loss and prevent the brittle bones and osteoporosis suffered by many women. What's more, recent studies suggest that a high calcium intake, particularly from low-fat dairy products, can help you lose weight! Researchers believe that calcium stored in fat cells helps promote fat burning. In one twenty-four-week study published in the *American Journal for Clinical Nutrition,* people who consumed three to four servings of low-fat dairy a day lost 10.9 percent of their body weight; and those who took calcium supplements lost 8.1 percent; others, with low calcium intakes, dropped only 6.4 percent. If you're lactose intolerant, try eating more calcium-fortified soy milk, orange juice, cereals, dark leafy greens, or sardines.

Actress Julianne Phillips, who starred in the TV show *Sisters,* used to pop a sweet potato in the oven before we began working out. We could actually smell it baking while we exercised. She said she knew she would be hungry after the session, and it helped to have a snack on deck. This way, once we were finished, it was ready to go.

How easy and nutritious can you get? Sweet potatoes are rich in beta-carotene and fiber, and they are delicious and satisfying. Pop one in the oven at 350° F. for 35 to 55 minutes, depending on its size. It will tide you over until your next meal and keep you away from fatty, sugary snacks.

- **Keep healthy snacks on hand.** Stock your refrigerator and pantry with nutritious nibbles, such as baby carrots, celery sticks, yogurt, air-popped popcorn, sliced turkey breast, hummus, whole wheat crackers, and fresh fruits. Also, keep a stash of snacks—like dried fruit, soy nuts, oat bran pretzels, or whole grain cereal—in your handbag, in your car, and at work.

- **Sit down when you eat.** It will force you to focus on your meal, not the ten other things you're trying to do at the same time, so you will feel more satisfied mentally and physically.

- **Eat slowly.** Try putting your fork down and counting to ten after each bite. It will help you slow down, so your brain has a chance to notify your stomach that you've eaten enough.

- **Satisfy your cravings.** Rather than ignoring your cravings (which is likely to backfire), try indulging in a moderate way. It's better to satisfy your desire for ice cream with a kiddie cone than to binge on an entire carton.

- **Don't eat late at night.** Nighttime is prime time for mindless eating. To keep fat and calories in check, limit predinner snacks to light, nutritious foods, such as raw vegetables with salsa. To prevent after-dinner snacking, immediately get up and brush your teeth after finishing your meal, chew gum, or sip herbal tea.

# The Recipe for a Healthy Lifestyle

Exercise and good eating are two important steps on the path to a better body. But they aren't the only steps! The following "must dos" will help make your journey down the healthy lifestyle highway complete:

**Get enough sleep.** Proper rest is necessary for a healthy body. When you're sleep-deprived you feel tired, lethargic, and cranky. Your skin looks dull. You may feel too tired to exercise. This fatigue often leads to poor food choices. You may turn to unnatural sources of energy, such as caffeine or sugary foods, for an energy boost.

**Limit alcohol.** Beer, wine, and mixed cocktails pack a high-calorie punch. Often we associate calories with food, and forget that the drink we're knocking back is loaded with calories. I recently read that the average-size frozen margarita has 550 calories! Since alcohol lowers your inhibitions, it can also cause you to overeat. While some studies have shown that one drink a day may have health benefits, any more than that could increase your risk of heart disease and breast cancer. So if you do choose to raise your glass, stick to a light beer, a glass of red wine, or a white wine spritzer.

**Minimize stress.** Chronic stress can be toxic. It can weaken your immune system and lead to serious problems such as hypertension, atherosclerosis, colitis, and depression. Research also strongly links stress to overeating and weight gain. Exercise is one of the most effective ways to reduce your stress level. Spending time with friends, listening to music, meditation, and deep breathing can also help you chill out.

**Don't smoke.** Smoking may look sexy on the silver screen, but it's one of the most damaging things you can do to your body. According to the Centers for Disease Control and Prevention (CDC), cigarette smoking causes approximately 400,000 deaths in the United States each year, making it the single most preventable cause of premature death. Women who smoke are twelve times more likely to die from lung cancer and three times more likely to die of heart disease. If you smoke, you're also at much higher risk of developing emphysema, cataracts, and osteoporosis—not to mention wrinkles, dirty teeth, and bad breath.

## Weighing In on the Scale

I'm constantly asked how much weight my celebrity clients have lost. While the number on the scale may mean a lot to some people, it isn't something that I focus on. First of all, it doesn't tell me anything about how your workouts are making you feel. Second, it isn't an accurate gauge of your fitness level or your body composition.

As I explained earlier, muscle weighs more than fat. So if you're losing fat and gaining muscle, your body weight may not change dramatically. But the reality is, you're getting leaner, slimmer, and firmer, and improving your health. Since our bodies are mostly water, the amount that you drink or perspire can also cause your weight to fluctuate from morning to evening. If you live and die by the scale, you may never have an accurate picture of the progress you are making.

Many of my clients, including Michelle Pfeiffer, have said good-bye to their scales. As Michelle puts it, why step on the scale and ruin your whole day? I couldn't agree more. Follow Michelle's lead and focus on how your clothes fit instead. If your pants are getting looser, then you're on track. If your pants feel tight, then you need to watch it.

Or, if you're addicted to numbers, get your body fat tested instead. A body-fat test looks at the composition of your entire body, focusing on lean body mass versus body fat. The test is simple and involves being pinched by "calipers" on the back of your arm, thigh, and hip. The measurements are then entered into a formula to determine your body-fat index. You can keep track of the results to measure your progress.

## Accepting Your Body Type

People often ask me, "If I do these exercises, will I look like Michelle Pfeiffer or Jennifer Aniston?" Sorry, but my answer is no. Genes play a major role in determining your physique, and you can't fight genetics. Some of us are pear shaped, some naturally thin, some curvy, some tall, and some petite. While you can significantly improve on what you have by eating right and exercising, you can't make your body look like someone else's.

Beauty comes in all shapes and sizes, and one of the most important steps to getting a body that you love is self-acceptance. That said, I know that it isn't always easy to feel good about your physique. Every day, we're bombarded with images of celebrities who look stunningly perfect in every way, shape, and form. Some look as if they don't have an ounce of fat on their bodies. Others may have sexy curves, but cellulite still seems to be nonexistent. Are these women for real? How can we ever measure up?

It's time to let you in on another little Hollywood secret. Many of the picture-perfect photos that you see in fashion magazines are digitally altered to remove any lumps, bumps, and imperfections. What's more, makeup artists, hair stylists, and wardrobe experts have spent hours working their magic. I'm not saying that these stars aren't gorgeous in real life, without computer airbrushing and makeup. But don't be fooled into thinking that they don't have flaws. Believe me, *no one* looks that way when they wake up in the morning!

Even my celebrity clients have insecurities about their bodies. They're afraid one area is too small or another area too big. They're nervous that they won't get a part or will lose a part if they don't look like a million bucks. The phrase "red carpet" sends terror through many . . . scrutiny by millions, not to mention Joan Rivers, the merciless host of E! Entertainment Television's *Fashion Police.* That would make anyone insecure!

I'll confess: When I first started working as a trainer in Hollywood, I felt self-conscious about my body. Los Angeles is the land of the beautiful, and everywhere you go you see thin, blond women who look like Barbie. Even though I was lean and toned, I thought I looked big, especially next to some of the tiny actresses that I was working with. My boyfriend at the time constantly told me that he loved my body. But I still had trouble accepting it. When I looked in the mirror, all I could see was my broad shoulders and muscular legs.

Finally, after a few years, I was able to stop the cycle of discontent. It took a while, but I stopped worrying about how I "should" look. I realized that it didn't matter what other people thought of me, as long as I felt good about myself. I guess I just got tired of beating myself up inside. I got tired of the constant comparisons and fretting over how different I looked from my glamorous clients. It was exhausting, all that self-doubt! These days, I feel so much more at peace with my body. I think it had a lot to do with becoming a mom. I no longer obsess over how I look in a bathing suit. Now, I care more about feeling strong, being healthy, maintaining my energy, and keeping up with my kids in a game of tag.

Starting today, I want you to do something that—coming from this book—may seem a bit counterintuitive: I want you to lose the "I want to look like her" mentality. The celebrities featured in this book are all beautiful, healthy women whose fitness habits are worth emulating. But you shouldn't compare yourself to them. It will do nothing but lead to frustration, despair, and low self-esteem. It's much more important to focus on your own fitness accomplishments as we work out together in the weeks ahead. Notice the sparkle in your eyes and the color in your cheeks. Feel the sexy muscles developing in your arms and legs. And most important, pay attention to how much better you feel about yourself.

## The Final Scene

In the quest for a better body, our biggest enemy is often ourselves. No, I'm not talking about a lack of willpower. I'm talking about the pressure that we put on ourselves to be perfect. We want all the body fat to disappear in a week. We feel like failures if we eat a slice of cake or miss a single workout. We get depressed if we don't look like supermodels or movie stars.

Before you get started, I want to remind you that realistic expectations are crucial to success. Change doesn't happen overnight. You can't expect the excess weight to fall off. So be patient! Even though you're transforming the way you eat and exercise, you must take it one step at a time. This is a lifestyle makeover, not a quick-fix exercise and diet plan. There is no "before" and "after."

As you embark on this new healthy lifestyle, it's also important to stay positive. If you truly believe that you can be successful, you'll have a much better chance of making a lasting change. I'm not saying that your transition to a regular exercise program and a healthy diet is going to be seamless. It will be easier on some days, and harder on others. So just do the best that you can. If you slip up, try to learn from your mistakes and stay focused on the next step. Fitness can be hard work, but it *really* pays off in the end.

Remember, what you see in the mirror is far less important than how you feel deep inside. Being happy from within gives you a glow that can't be beat! So don't keep dwelling on your flaws or wishing that you looked like a swimsuit model. Accept what you can't change, and work on changing what you can. Instead of striving for perfection, work on feeling comfortable in your own skin and getting into the best shape of your life.

# CHAPTER TWO

# The Opening Scene
# . . . or, Getting Started

*I* *n the twenty-plus years that I've worked as a* personal trainer, I've loved helping people change their bodies and lives through fitness. Nothing makes me happier than seeing my clients transform themselves from tired women in lackluster shape to positive, energized, and fit females. Whether I'm working out with an Oscar-winning actress, a top supermodel, or one of my neighborhood moms, it's so incredibly rewarding to watch her confidence grow with each new achievement.

We all want to feel good about ourselves, whether we're walking down a red carpet or down the supermarket aisle, into a job interview, or onto a movie set. Even if you're not posing for cameras or being pursued by the paparazzi, you deserve to look and feel your best at all times. In the

## Your Weekly Workout Schedule

**Monday:** The Supermodel Lower-Body Conditioner (55 minutes)

**Tuesday:** Rachel's Super-Sexy Upper Body–Sculpting Workout (25 minutes), plus The Amazing Abs Bonus Workout (5 minutes)

**Wednesday:** The Hidden Hills Workout (25 minutes)

**Thursday:** The Pretty Woman Leg Workout (25 minutes), plus The Amazing Abs Bonus Workout (5 minutes)

**Friday:** The Charlie's Angels Boot Camp Workout (50 minutes)

**Saturday or Sunday:** The Amazing Abs Bonus Workout (5 minutes)

following pages, you'll learn more about the Hollywood workouts that will help you build a lean, firm, healthy body that you love. With my weekly plan, you can minimize flab, tone your trouble spots, and improve your posture, coordination, and balance. You'll also experience what I call the "icing on the cake" benefits—more energy, better self-esteem, and a positive outlook.

Best of all, you can accomplish all of this in less than an hour a day, five to six days a week. Trust me! My celebrity clients have crazy schedules just like you, and they don't want to work out a minute longer than they have to. I've tailored these routines to deliver maximum results with a minimum of effort. A few of the workouts are longer—50 to 55 minutes—but some are less: just 25 minutes. String them together and you'll be exercising for roughly three and a half hours a week—that's an average of only 30 minutes a day. That's not so bad!

## How This Program Works

The five innovative workouts in Chapters 4 through 8 will form the foundation of your weekly plan. Each workout features the body-sculpting exercises and calorie-blasting cardio routines that I've used with Claudia Schiffer, Jennifer Aniston, Julia Roberts, Drew Barrymore, and other famous clients. In Chapter 9, you'll find a bonus workout with ab-blasting exercises that I did with supermodel Cindy Crawford, which should be incorporated into your program three times a week. Put them all together and you've got a week's worth of workouts designed to strengthen and chisel you from head to toe.

On page 27, I've provided a weekly workout schedule for you to follow. Or you can create a customized plan by selecting workouts that coincide with your timetable, mood, and energy level. For example, if you take night classes on Wednesdays, you can move the Wednesday workout to Saturday. If Tuesday is your day off, you can push the Tuesday workout to Sunday and enjoy your free day doing an activity you love. Switching the order of your workouts won't hinder your success. Creating a schedule that works for you is the most important thing.

If you're anything like the celebrities I work with, you may get bored doing the same routine over and over and over again. That's one of the reasons why I've incorporated so much variety into this weeklong program. By doing a wide range of exercises and activities, you'll also force your body to work harder and activate more muscles for a bigger calorie burn and better overall conditioning. I call it the "buffet" approach to fitness—but don't worry, you won't gain an ounce! Instead, you'll see your body take on a whole new shape, complete with toned and sculpted muscles.

Each strength workout should begin with a short warm-up and end with the cool-down stretches provided. To reduce your risk of injury, it's crucial that your muscles, ligaments, and tendons are warm before you get started. Stretching at the end of your workouts will help keep your muscles limber and hasten your recovery. As I explained earlier, some research suggests that stretching can also help you build strength and muscle faster—and the faster you build muscle, the faster you'll increase your metabolism. End result: better muscle tone and less body fat.

This weekly program is geared toward regular exercisers. If it's been more than a month since your last workout—regardless of whether you've been laid up with an injury, recently had a baby, or haven't moved since your junior high P.E. class—you'll need to ease into it. That's where Chapter 3's Early Morning Start-up Workout comes in. Inspired by my longtime client Michelle Pfeiffer, the two-week plan is designed to help you gradually and safely develop strength and endurance. It includes both a cardio and strength workout, each of which should be performed three times a week. After completing this basic start-up program, you should be ready to progress to the main program.

If you're starting an exercise program for the first time or coming off a long hiatus, it's wise to check with your doctor before getting started. As a general rule, I recommend seeing your primary care physician once a year for a basic physical. Even if you feel healthy, it's important to get your cholesterol, blood pressure, and blood sugar levels checked to screen for heart disease, diabetes, and other serious problems. In addition, you should discuss your family health history and any concerns or abnormal symptoms that you're having. So use this as the impetus you need to schedule that appointment!

If the exercise routines seem difficult or you feel uncoordinated at first, don't get discouraged! Whenever you try something new, it takes time for your body to learn and adjust. Even my celebrity clients have a tough time stringing all the moves together perfectly at first. As you develop strength, balance, and agility, the cardio and strength routines will become easier—I promise. You'll feel less like a clumsy beginner and more like an old pro. And you'll soon discover a sense of balance and agility you didn't know you had.

Your workouts should be challenging, but not so taxing that you hurt yourself or hate every minute of them. So listen to your body. If it's telling you to slow down or use lighter weights, pay attention. If five days a week is too much in the beginning, scale back to three or four days until you feel ready for more. Try to find that place between "too hard" and "not hard enough." If you run out of steam before the end of your cardio workout, that's OK. Just do the best that you can, and strive to do even better next time. And if you feel any pain, stop immediately. Consult your physician if you have a pain that lasts more than a few days.

With any fitness plan, flexibility is key to success. Though I've supplied structured workouts, you should feel free to adapt them to meet your individual needs. For example, if you have time constraints, you may want to split your workouts into shorter sessions and do them at different times of day. Instead of doing a full 30 minutes of cardio, you can do half in the morning and half before dinner. Or divide a 25-minute strength-training routine into five 5-minute segments. When it comes to burning calories and getting in better shape, these smaller bits of activity definitely add up!

Before starting, take a look at your calendar to determine the best time of day for you to exercise. It's a good idea to plan your workouts at the same time every day, so you get into a routine. If you're a working girl and don't have to be in the office until 9 A.M., early mornings might be your best bet. If you're a mom trying to get kids out the door for school, late morning or early afternoon may be more realistic. There is no right or wrong answer about when to work out. All that matters is that you pick a time that you'll stick with.

If you follow this program consistently, you should begin to see dramatic improvements in strength, aerobic capacity, and body composition in about eight to twelve weeks. Since all of our bodies respond to exercise differently, some of you will get results more quickly. But most important,

# Seared Carpaccio of Beef with Roasted Baby Beets, Creamed Horseradish, Watercress, and Parmesan

Adopting a healthy lifestyle doesn't have to mean giving up special-occasion meals. Here, my *Today* show colleague Jamie Oliver, a.k.a. the Naked Chef, has provided a recipe for a nutritious meal so rich and robust that you'll fool your guests into thinking it's totally sinful. In reality, filet of beef is one of the leanest, protein-rich cuts of red meat. Add beets, which are an excellent source of calcium, iron, and beta-carotene, and the kick of horseradish, and you have a magnificent and healthy meal.

**Makes 4 servings**

2 pounds baby beetroots
Olive oil
10 tablespoons balsamic vinegar
Salt and freshly ground black pepper

1 heaped tablespoon coriander seeds, smashed
1 handful of fresh rosemary, finely chopped
Salt and freshly ground black pepper
A light sprinkling of dried oregano
2 pounds fillet of beef

2 ounces freshly grated or creamed horseradish
7 ounces crème fraîche
A splash of white wine vinegar, or juice of 1 lemon
3 good handfuls of watercress
2 ounces shaved Parmesan cheese

Preheat the oven to 450°F.

**For the beets:** Wash and scrub the beets, trim the ends, and toss into a roasting tray with a little olive oil, the balsamic vinegar, salt, and pepper. Cover with kitchen foil and roast until tender. Cooking time depends on size.

**For the beef:** Pound the coriander seeds in a pestle and mortar, then mix in the rosemary, salt, pepper, and oregano and sprinkle onto a board. Roll and press the fillet of beef over this, making sure all the mixture sticks to the meat. In a very hot, ridged pan, or on a barbecue, sear the meat for about 5 minutes until brown and slightly crisp on all sides. Remove from the pan. Allow it to rest for 5 minutes, then slice it all up as thinly as you can. Lay the slices on a large plate.

After preparing the beef, sprinkle the roasted beetroots randomly (whole, halved, or quartered, depending on size) over the sliced meat. In a small to medium bowl, mix the horseradish and crème fraîche together. It has to be seasoned well, usually needing a little white wine vinegar or lemon juice. Dribble this over the beetroots. Dress some watercress with olive oil and lemon juice. Then scatter this, along with some small slivers of shaved Parmesan, all over the plate and get ready to tuck in!

Reprinted with permission from *The Naked Chef Takes Off,* copyright © 2002, Hyperion Books.

all of you should notice changes in your attitude, mood, confidence, sleeping patterns, and overall well-being right away.

You've heard me say repeatedly that this is a lifestyle change, not a get-fit-quick scheme. So don't plan to exercise your butt off for a month and then place this book on a shelf to collect dust. I've seen remarkable physical and psychological transformations with my clients, but only with those who are faithful to their workouts. Without consistency, there's no guarantee that you'll experience all of the benefits I described earlier. It's up to you to make the commitment and make fitness a priority.

Don't forget, as we discussed in the previous chapter, exercise and healthy eating go hand in hand when it comes to getting visible results. If your diet consists of hot dogs, Krispy Kremes, and mocha lattes, you won't see the same improvement as someone who is also watching what she eats. For some of you, your food choices may be nutritious, but you're still eating too much. If so, now is the time to transition to proper portion sizes. Good nutrition and portion control is crucial when you're attempting to create a caloric deficit and slim down.

For maximum benefits, you should also try to stay as active as possible throughout the day. As I explained in Chapter 1, the more you move, the more calories your body will burn, the more energy you'll have, and the happier and healthier you will be. During the week, you can squeeze more activity in by walking more, taking the stairs, and just standing up and stretching. Weekends are wonderful opportunities to try some new recreational activities—or return to some old favorites. Take a bike ride. Play eighteen holes of golf (no carts, please!). Go for a swim. Try snowboarding or waterskiing. Use your newfound fitness to explore a hiking trail or participate in the local "fun run." It doesn't matter what you do—just do it!

Are you ready to get going? I am! Here's what you'll need to get started . . .

## Your Fitness Toolbox

What follows is a checklist of all the inexpensive but effective tools that you'll need for your workouts. Some of them are objects that you may already have around the house. Unless otherwise noted, the rest can be purchased from your local sporting goods store, Target, Wal-Mart, and fitness retailers such as SPRI International (800-222-7774; www.spriproducts.com), and Exertools (800-235-1559; www.exer-tools.com). If you're on a tight budget, you may want to look for used fitness equipment at garage sales or on eBay (www.ebay.com). Or try placing a classified ad in your local newspaper.

Jump rope: Jumping rope is one of my all-time favorite cardio workouts. It not only burns a lot of calories, it's great for toning your butt, legs, arms, and shoulders. My favorite jump rope, called the Animal, costs about $25 and is available from Super Rope, Inc. (414-771-0849).

Dumbbells: In order to get stronger and achieve the toned, sculpted look that my celebrity clients have, you need to use some form of resistance to challenge your muscles. For some strength exercises, you'll be using your body weight for resistance. For others, you'll need three pairs of dumbbells, in 3-, 5- and 8-pound increments. Dumbbells are usually priced between $10 and $25 per pair, depending on the weight and materials used. While you can use water bottles, soup cans, or similar household items, I strongly urge you to invest in a set of dumbbells. It's really a small price to pay for a strong, lean body!

Stability ball: Some of the strength moves in this program are performed either sitting or lying on a large exercise ball, also known as a stability ball, Swiss ball, or physioball. You've likely seen these large inflatable balls, which look like giant versions of the balls we played with as kids. By doing the exercises on an unstable surface, you can strengthen your core muscles (your abs and back) while improving your balance, agility, and posture. A stability ball is multifunctional, easy to store, and costs only about $20 to $30. The balls come in different sizes, and it's important to use one that's appropriate for your height. (When you're seated on top of the ball, your knees should be bent at about a 90-degree angle.) If you're between 5′0″ and 5′7″, you'll need a 55-centimeter ball. If you're taller than 5′8″, opt for a 65-centimeter ball. If you're under 5′0″, choose a 45-centimeter ball. Be sure to purchase a ball made with antiburst material, and fully inflate it before you begin.

**Medium-sized ball:**   Any type of light ball, such as a basketball, soccer ball, volleyball, dodgeball, or small beach ball, will do the trick.

**Watch with a timer:**   All of the cardio workouts in this program consist of timed intervals. To time yourself, I recommend using a digital sports watch, such as the Women's Timex Ironman Triathlon Digital Watch, which retails for about $50. You could also use a stopwatch, such as the one made by Sportline, which costs less than $20. Or, any watch with a second hand will work in a pinch.

**Sturdy chair:**   For exercises that call for a chair, you can use any stable kitchen or dining room chair without arms, and with a chair back that you can hold on to.

**Wastebasket:**   If you don't have one, you can use a laundry basket, a medium-sized box, or a stack of towels instead.

**Small towel**

**Masking tape**

**Deck of cards**

For your workouts, you'll also need two platforms that you can safely stand on, as follows:

**Low platform:**   About 1 to 2 inches high. You can use anything from a step aerobics bench to two hardcover coffee table books.

**High platform:**   About 12 inches high. You can use a sturdy low chair, step stool or bench, or a step aerobics bench with three risers.

Optional:

**Exercise mat:**   If you're doing your strength exercises on a hard floor, you may want to use an exercise mat for cushioning. If you don't have a mat, use a bath towel instead.

**Pillow:**   Any standard pillow will do.

**Step aerobics bench:**   While it isn't essential for this program, a step bench, like the ones used in step aerobics classes, is a good piece of equipment to have around. You can use it for the exercises in this book that require a platform. Or you can purchase a step aerobics video and get a cardio workout. The Original Health Club Step, which comes with two risers, retails for about $105, but I've seen it for less.

## 6 Simple Workout Tips

If I were standing next to you during your workouts, you'd probably hear each of the following tips at least once. Keep them in mind in the coming weeks to get the most out of your exercise sessions and maximize your results.

### Breathe!

It may sound obvious, but many people forget to breathe during their strength routines. Deep breathing can help you relax and keep you from tensing your muscles. It also helps pump oxygen into your system, delivering fresh nutrients to your muscles and reducing fatigue. As you do each move, you should exhale on the "exertion," or lifting of the weight, and inhale on the "extension," or lowering of the weight.

### Watch Your Form

Good form is essential for optimal benefits and avoiding injuries. During your strength workouts, you should stand or sit tall, with your chest muscles lifted, your belly button pulled in, and your shoulders relaxed (not hunched). Perform each exercise slowly and with complete control. Don't swing the weights or allow momentum to take over.

### Use the Right Resistance

Your weights should be heavy enough that your muscles feel fatigued by the last few repetitions, but not so heavy that you sacrifice your form or feel muscle or joint strain. As you get stronger, you may want to increase the amount of resistance you're using so your muscles stay challenged. But never lift a weight that you don't feel comfortable with.

# Commit to Getting Fit

Congratulations again! You've made the important decision to start taking care of your body. Now take a minute to make a written contract with yourself. Start by writing down your reasons for wanting to make this healthy change and how it will help improve the quality of your life. Then, sign and date it at the bottom. Place this pledge on your nightstand and read it every morning before getting out of bed. Or carry it with you and whip it out whenever you feel tempted to skip a workout.

Signature _____     Date _____

## Pace Yourself

You should always be able to speak comfortably during your cardio sessions. If you're red in the face and gasping for air, you're overdoing it! Likewise, if your breathing isn't heavy and labored, you aren't working hard enough. As you build cardiovascular strength, you'll need to push yourself a little harder so your progress continues, but not so hard that you can't catch your breath.

## Progress Slowly

When it comes to fitness, slow and steady wins the race! To keep your muscles fresh and your motivation high, you should work on increasing strength and endurance in small increments. If you don't give your body enough rest, you won't progress as quickly, and you're apt to burn out. If you miss several workouts in a row, be sure to ease back into your routine. One power session won't make up for lost time.

## Dress for Success

Comfortable clothing and footwear can mean the difference between an invigorating workout and quitting early. So be sure your clothes aren't too tight or too loose; they should allow you to move freely, but not be so baggy that they get in the way. I love the feel of cotton, while some of my clients swear by Lycra and other sweat-wicking fabrics. Find what works for you! Your sneakers should have plenty of support and cushion. If they're showing signs of wear, it's time for a new pair.

# The Early Morning Start-up Workout

## . . . Starring Michelle Pfeiffer

*W*hen Catwoman, a.k.a Michelle Pfeiffer, called me in 1991, I almost couldn't believe this gorgeous screen star needed a personal trainer. I'd seen her in *The Fabulous Baker Boys, Dangerous Liaisons,* and *Tequila Sunrise,* and as far as I could tell, she was in great shape. She looked stunning in every role that she played. But as you'll learn, looks can be deceiving.

It was late in the summer, and Michelle had already started filming *Batman Returns.* Sure, she wanted to look toned and trim in her sexy vinyl cat suit. But she also needed to improve her strength for the physically demanding role. Since Michelle hadn't been exercising consistently, she had quite a bit of work to do to get ready for her action-packed part.

Michelle needed to be on the set and ready for hair and makeup by six o'clock every morning. So our daily workouts were scheduled for 4:30 A.M. at her home. At that hour of the day, it can be difficult to keep your eyes open, much less engage in stimulating conversation. There wasn't a whole lot of talking, but that was a good thing in a way. We usually got right down to business.

Michelle's mission-style home was located in Brentwood, the Los Angeles suburb made famous by the O. J. Simpson murder trial. I used a security code to enter, so I didn't have to ring the doorbell and wake the entire house. On a typical morning, I'd be walking over to Michelle's exercise mat just as she entered the living room. We'd mutter a sleepy "Hey," exchange smiles, turn on music, and get started. Michelle usually wore a

## Workout Sneak Preview

If you haven't been exercising regularly, Michelle's Early Morning Start-up Workout will be the first important step on your road to a better body. This two-week program is designed to help you ease back into a fitness program and build a foundation of endurance and strength, just as Michelle Pfeiffer did before her role in the blockbuster film *Batman Returns.*

Working out at 4:30 A.M. may sound crazy to you, but it's a coveted time slot for many of my clients. At least twice a week, actress Alfre Woodard and I go walking on the beach in Santa Monica before the sun rises, and Meg Ryan and I used to jog through the streets of Brentwood before most people see the light of day.

pair of sweats or bike shorts and a T-shirt, with her hair pulled back into a ponytail. I was relieved to see that, like me, she looked like she had just rolled out of bed!

Despite her good intentions, Michelle had never been able to maintain a regular exercise program—at least not for the long haul. She would work out for a few weeks or months at a time, then stop for a while. (Sound familiar?) So she needed to work on building up her strength and endurance, and getting her body back into the exercise groove. It was also important for her to find an exercise routine that she enjoyed. During the first several weeks, we focused on developing muscular strength, increasing stamina, burning calories, and invigorating her body. These workouts were basic, but they were effective.

Over time, as Michelle got stronger, we adjusted her program accordingly, and she added more equipment, from stretch bands to dumbbells to a stationary bike to her fitness toolbox. As I told Michelle, if you're coming off a fitness hiatus, it's important to take it slow in the beginning. If you try to do too much, too soon, you're apt to end up frustrated, sore, or with a painful injury, which could derail your motivation and cause you to quit.

I also talked to Michelle about her eating habits, as I do with all of my clients. She was already very committed to good nutrition. She ate a lot of fish and steamed vegetables and, for a vitamin-enriched snack, she often had a PowerBar. Although her diet was healthy and balanced, she wasn't overly rigid about what she ate. She still allowed herself an occasional splurge. For instance, at the movies she liked putting M&M's into her popcorn. I know it sounds bizarre, but she liked the salty-sweet combination. Plus, she loved how the warm popcorn melted the chocolate a bit.

When trying to lose weight or get more defined, many people tell themselves that they can never eat certain foods again. But I've found that this kind of restrictive dieting only causes you to obsess about food. When you finally give in to your cravings (which is almost guaranteed to happen), you're apt to devour twice as much of these "off limits" foods, then feel like a failure—or worse, give up on healthy eating altogether. Instead, I believe it's better to be realistic, reasonable, and relaxed about your diet. It's OK to indulge once in a while, as long as you do so in moderation. If you're going to have a treat, keep it small, savor every bite, and balance it out by eating nutritious foods the rest of the day.

When the filming of *Batman Returns* ended, Michelle and I switched our workout time to 6 A.M. After those 4:30 A.M. sessions, it felt like sleeping in! By that point, it was obvious that Michelle's hard work and dedication were paying off. She was much stronger. I could push her much harder than I could in the beginning. And she could work out for

## Create Your Own Gym, Michelle Pfeiffer-Style!

During the filming of *Batman Returns,* we worked out in Michelle's living room. But once she decided to stick with exercise, she turned her garage into a home gym. You can, too—and it doesn't have to cost a lot of money. Michelle divided her two-car garage in half and put drywall in the middle. Then she threw down some indoor/outdoor carpeting. (You could also use astroturf or flat, gray industrial carpet.) She plugged in her treadmill and put mirrors along one wall. You can pick up two or three full-length mirrors at Target or Home Depot and hang them side by side. *Voilà!* Add an exercise mat, hand weights and other tools, and a CD player or television, and you've got your own private exercise studio. Having a designated "workout space" in your home can be very motivating. Every time you walk by, you're reminded to get in there and move! Plus, it shows that you're committed to getting fit. If you don't have a garage, use a spare bedroom or a corner of your basement, living room, or den instead. To keep it tidy, try storing your workout tools, such as resistance bands, weights, a jump rope, and videotapes, in a large basket.

longer periods of time. It just goes to show what a difference a well-designed exercise program—and consistency—can make.

Now, more than a decade later, Michelle has managed to turn those crack-of-dawn exercise sessions into a habit. While she admits that working out can still be a chore, she has continued to stick with it. Now that she has two kids, the early morning, when her kids are still sleeping, is often the only time she can squeeze fitness into her schedule. What's more, it helps her wake up and gives her energy for the rest of her day. Perhaps best of all, when you exercise in the morning, you get your workout over with. Leaving it until the afternoon or evening can be risky because, as we all know, there are dozens of other activities and commitments that can get in the way. At the end of a long day, it's only too easy to tell yourself, "Oh, I'm just too tired!" or "I'll save my workout for tomorrow."

## Turning Back the Clock

If you aren't a morning person, I honestly believe that you can train yourself to be one. It's simply a matter of changing your lifestyle and resetting your internal clock. When I began working with actress Penelope Ann Miller, she was a serious night owl. She didn't go to bed until 2 or 3 A.M., then she'd sleep until noon. I had trouble scheduling her into my training roster, because she wanted to work out in the midafternoon. (I typically book my clients in the morning, and by three in the afternoon I'm wiped out!) Since then, Penelope's adopted a dog, gotten married, and had a baby. Needless to say, her schedule has changed dramatically. She now goes to bed early and gets up early. These days, our one-on-one sessions take place at 9 A.M. sharp. Her body has adjusted to her new routine, and yours will, too. Remember: If you get out of bed and exercise bright and early, you won't have all day to dream up excuses to skip your workout.

## Breakfast—To Eat or Not to Eat?

Michelle didn't eat anything before our predawn workouts, and neither did I. But some of you may need a little fuel to get you started and help maximize your workout. If so, try having a glass of orange juice diluted with water, a piece of whole wheat toast with a dab of peanut butter, or half a banana for a quick boost of energy. Keep in mind: Whenever you eat before a workout, you should keep it light, or after a larger meal, leave enough time to digest. No matter when you choose to exercise, you never want to do it on a full stomach. If you eat too much, you're apt to feel lethargic or get a cramp.

While Michelle's Early Morning Start-up Workout can be performed at any time of day, I recommend doing it early, before work and while your kids are still in bed, just like Michelle. It will help you start your day on the right foot, get into a routine, and minimize the blow-off potential. Of course, the hardest part will probably be getting up and moving. So before you go to sleep, be sure all of your workout tools are out and ready. Set your alarm a little earlier than you normally would, and try either sleeping in your workout clothes or laying them out right next to your bed. When your alarm goes off, the last thing that you're going to want to do is exercise. Having everything prepared to go to will help make your transition from sleeping beauty to A.M. exerciser as easy as possible. Later in the day, you'll be happy that you did!

# Michelle's Early Morning Start-up Workout

**THE PLAN**

Do both the cardio and strength workouts three times a week. **For cardio:** To increase your stamina, enhance your energy, and burn calories, you'll be doing a mile of brisk walking, trying to go a little faster each time. **For strength:** To boost muscular strength, balance, and coordination, you'll do a 20-minute mix of traditional strength moves, ballet, and plyometrics. (Plyometrics are "explosive" moves that involve stretching a muscle before contracting it, to increase strength and power.) With this effective but not-too-strenuous workout, you'll work major muscle groups in your upper and lower body, and start the process of getting back into shape.

You can perform these two programs back-to-back or split them up between morning and evening. Or do them on alternate days. (For example, strength on Monday, Wednesdays, and Fridays; cardio on Tuesdays, Thursdays, and Saturdays.) To give your muscles time to recover, be sure to take a rest day between strength workouts. Follow this program for two weeks, then advance to the main plan (see Chapter 2 for details).

### What You'll Need

- Watch with a timer
- Sturdy chair
- Masking tape
- Dumbbells (3 to 5 pounds)
- Towel
- Exercise mat (optional)

The goal of this cardio workout is to walk one mile in 15 minutes or less. If you can't walk a 15-minute mile, you'll need to work on gradually increasing your speed. (Use the sample cardio schedule below as a guide.) If you can already walk a 15-minute mile, continue working on picking up the pace. If you feel ready, try alternating spurts of fast walking and slow jogging. But don't overdo it! As I said earlier, if you push yourself too hard, you can end up sore or injured, which in turn could soften your resolve and jeopardize your fitness goals. It's better to work on slowly building speed and endurance.

If you plan to walk outside, start by getting in the car and clocking a mile-long route. (While you're doing this, you also may want to map out 1.5- and 2-mile routes, which you'll be using for The Supermodel Lower-Body Conditioner and Charlie's Angels' Boot Camp Workout.) Another option is to use your local high school track (four laps equal one mile).

If your climate isn't conducive to exercising outdoors, you can walk on a treadmill or possibly at your local shopping mall. (At some malls, you can get inside early, before stores open, to walk. Some malls also provide a map with distances. Check with your nearby shopping center to find out whether these perks are available.) To time yourself, use a watch with a timer or a stopwatch. Be sure to wear comfortable walking shoes or cross trainers on your feet.

## Berry Smooth Smoothie

I love starting my day with a smoothie! This Berry Smooth Smoothie, one of my very favorites, is rich in vitamin C and calcium. You can use any type of frozen or fresh fruit in place of or in addition to the strawberries. Add half a banana to make it more creamy, or a splash of nonfat milk or orange juice to thin it. You can also substitute non- or low-fat vanilla yogurt for the plain yogurt, vanilla, and sugar.                    **Makes 1 serving**

**¾ cup frozen unsweetened strawberries**          **1 teaspoon sugar**
**½ cup plain low-fat yogurt**                               **A few ice cubes**
**1 teaspoon vanilla extract**

Put all of the ingredients in a blender and blend at low speed until smooth.

### Sample Cardio Schedule

**Week 1**

    Monday: Walk one mile at a 22 minutes/mile pace

    Wednesday: Walk one mile at a 20 minutes/mile pace

    Friday: Walk one mile at an 18 minutes/mile pace

**Week 2**

    Monday: Walk one mile at an 18 minutes/mile pace

    Wednesday: Walk one mile at a 16 minutes/mile pace

    Friday: Walk one mile at a 15 minutes/mile pace

**STRENGTH**

Do this strength workout three times a week, taking a rest day between training sessions. If you do these moves immediately following your cardio workout, you can skip the warm-up. End each workout by doing the cool-down stretches on pages 58–61. You should rest 15 to 60 seconds between exercises, depending on how fatigued you feel.

### The Warm-up

**March in Place.** Stand with your feet hip-width apart, arms by your sides. Keeping your chest lifted and belly button pulled in, lift one knee at a time as high as possible while swinging your arms, elbows bent at 90 degrees. Continue for 1 minute.

**Imaginary Jump Rope.** Jump with both feet together, keeping them low to the ground. Rotate your lower arms in small circles, keeping your upper arms and elbows stable, to turn your imaginary rope. Continue for 1 minute.

Repeat both moves, and you should be ready to start your workout.

## The Workout

**1. Chair Tap with Biceps Curls.**  Stand facing a sturdy chair (you can also use a coffee table or a bench). Keep your back straight, chest lifted, belly button pulled in, arms by your sides. Exhale as you lift your right foot and tap the chair seat, simultaneously bending your elbows to lift your hands up toward your shoulders in a biceps curl, palms facing up. Inhale as you lower foot and hands to starting position, then repeat with left foot. Continue alternating sides until you've done 20 taps with each foot. *Targets quadriceps, hamstrings, buttocks, biceps.*

**2. Sit-down Squat.** *To make this exercise easier, use a taller chair. To make it more challenging, use a shorter chair, stand with each foot on a book, or hold a 3- to 5-pound dumbbell in each hand.* Turn around, so your back is facing the chair seat, then stand with your feet hip-width apart, arms by your sides. Keeping your belly button pulled in, tailbone pointing down, and weight on your heels, exhale as you slowly bend your knees and slowly lower yourself down to the chair seat, simultaneously extending both arms in front of you at shoulder height. (If you're holding weights, leave your arms by your sides.) Gently tap the seat of the chair with your buttocks, then inhale as you slowly return to starting position. Take about 2 counts to lower and 2 counts to come back up. Do this 10 times. *Targets quadriceps, hamstrings, buttocks.*

**3. Basic Plié.** Stand with your feet separated about 2½ to 3 feet apart, knees slightly bent, feet slightly turned out, hands on hips. Keeping your chest lifted, belly button pulled in, and tailbone pointing down, exhale as you bend your knees to lower your hips into a plié, knees directly over your toes. (If your knees aren't in line with your toes, move your feet a little closer together.) Inhale, then exhale and squeeze your buttocks together as you straighten your legs to return to starting position. Do 15 pliés. Rest for 30 seconds, then repeat. *Targets buttocks, hamstrings, quadriceps, inner thighs.*

**4. Side-to-side Hop Step.** Take a long piece of masking tape and tape it to the floor in a vertical line. Stand to the left side of the tape with your feet together, arms by your sides, belly button pulled in. Hop with your right foot, then your left foot, over the tape, exhaling each time you push off your feet, landing with your knees slightly bent. Repeat the move, hopping to the left. Continue alternating sides until you've done a total of 20 hops in each direction. *Strengthens your heart and legs; improves coordination and balance.*

**5. Stationary Lunge.** *For a greater challenge, hold a 3- to 5-pound dumbbell in each hand.* Stand with your feet hip-width apart, chest lifted and belly button pulled in. Take a large step forward with your right foot, so your legs are in a wide split stance. Keeping your chest up and belly button in, exhale as you bend both knees into a lunge, so your right knee is directly over your right ankle and your left knee points to the floor, with your left heel lifted. (To make this move easier, don't bend your knees as much.) Inhale as you straighten both legs back to a standing position, remaining in a split stance, with your left heel lifted. Do 10 lunges with your right leg in front, then switch legs and repeat. *Targets buttocks, quadriceps, hamstrings.*

**6. Wall Run.** Stand facing a wall with your chest lifted and belly button pulled in. Take a large step back, so you're about an arm's length from the wall. Lean forward and place your hands shoulder-width apart on the wall at shoulder height, balancing on the balls of your feet. Keeping your elbows slightly bent and your torso slightly leaning forward, run in place, lifting your knees as high as you can, while pushing your hands against the wall. Count to 20 (10 knee lifts on each side). Rest for 30 to 60 seconds. Repeat 5 times. *Targets buttocks, hamstrings, quadriceps; boosts your heart rate.*

**7. Shoulder Touch and Reach.** Sit on your chair with your feet flat on the floor, your chest lifted, and your belly button pulled in. Place your hands on your shoulders, with your elbows bent and turned out to the sides. Exhale as you extend both arms up overhead, reaching up as far as you can. Slowly lower your hands to your shoulders. Do this 20 times. At the end, let your upper body collapse over your thighs and your arms dangle. Repeat the entire exercise once. *Targets shoulders.*

## The Power of Push-ups

Push-ups can be hard—I'll admit it. But they're one of my favorite exercises because you just can't beat the results: superdefined shoulders, chest, and triceps. No other exercise does as much in so little time. Plus, you don't need any equipment, so you can do them anywhere, from your office to a hotel room. Whenever you have a minute to spare, you can drop and do 10 or 15 push-ups. As you get stronger, try doing them with the tops of your feet on a chair seat or a stability ball for an added challenge. Or place one hand on a medium-sized ball to create instability. Your upper body will thank you!

**8. Push-up Proper.** From a kneeling position, lean forward and place your hands on the floor slightly wider than shoulder-width apart. With your arms supporting your body, squeeze your abs and buttocks so that your body forms a straight line from head to knees. Keeping your back straight and belly button pulled in, exhale as you slowly bend your arms to lower your chest until your upper arms are parallel to the floor. Inhale, then exhale as you use your chest and arm muscles to push back up to starting position. Start by doing this 3 to 5 times. Each training session, try to do a few more. And don't forget to breathe! Once you can comfortably do 15 consecutive bent-knee push-ups using proper form, try switching to a straight-leg push-up, with your legs extended straight behind you and your body weight resting on your toes. If lowering down is too difficult, hold your body in the "up" part of the push-up for as long as you can without sacrificing your form. *Targets chest, shoulders, triceps; core muscles work to stabilize your body.*

**9. Superman Meets Catwoman.** Lie facedown on the floor with your arms and legs extended, feet about six inches apart, belly button pulled in toward your spine. Lift your head and look down at the floor to keep your neck in a neutral position. Squeeze your buttocks as you slowly raise your arms, shoulders, and legs up to six inches off the floor. Hold for 5 counts, then lower to starting position. Do this 10 times. If this is too difficult, split it up so that you're lifting your upper body first, then your lower body. *Targets lower back, buttocks, hamstrings.*

## Banana Date Shake

Filled with potassium and calcium, Hollis Wilder's Banana Date Shake is a perfect pick-me-up after a morning workout, or a naturally sweet and satisfying midafternoon snack.      **Makes 1 serving**

¾ cup soy milk
1 frozen banana

3 large dates, seeds removed
A few ice cubes

Put all of the ingredients in a blender and blend at low speed until thick and creamy.

**10. Bicycle.** Lie on your back with your knees bent, lower back pressed into the floor. Rest your hands behind your head. Keeping your belly button pulled in, exhale as you extend your right leg out straight; simultaneously lift your shoulders off the floor and bring your right elbow and left knee toward each other. Inhale, then exhale as you repeat the exercise, using the opposite arm and leg. Keep the movement slow and controlled, and focus on using your abdominal muscles, not your legs or shoulders, to do the work. Continue alternating sides until you have done 10 on each side. Rest for 30 seconds, then repeat. *Targets abdominals (rectus abdominis, inner and outer obliques).*

## Cool-Down Stretches

**Standing Side Stretch.**  Stand with your feet hip-width apart, arms by your sides, belly button pulled in. Keeping your torso erect, inhale as you extend your left arm overhead, then reach it over the top of your head and to the left. Exhale as you feel the stretch along the right side of your body. Breathe deeply as you hold the stretch for 30 seconds, or as long as you can, without bouncing. Switch sides and repeat. *Stretches shoulders, waist, hips.*

**Chest Opener.** Stand with your feet hip-width apart, hands clasped behind you, chest lifted, and belly button pulled in. Keeping your arms straight, inhale as you lift your hands back and up behind you. Exhale as you feel your chest open. Breathe deeply as you hold the stretch for 30 seconds, or as long as you can, without bouncing. *Stretches chest.*

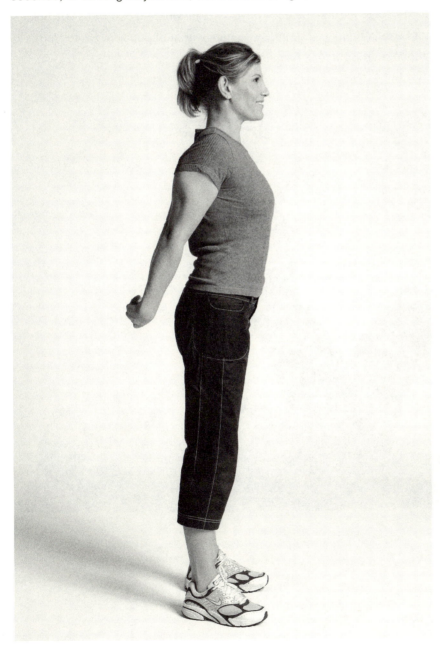

**Hamstring Stretch with Towel.** Lie on your back with your knees bent, feet flat on the floor. Hold one end of the towel in each hand, and hook the middle of the towel over the arch of your right foot. Now, extend your left leg straight up into the air, so it's slightly in front of your right hip. Exhale as you gently pull your left foot down toward you, using the towel to stretch the back of your thigh. Breathe deeply as you hold for 30 seconds, or as long as you can, without bouncing. Switch legs and repeat. *Stretches hamstrings.*

**Child's Pose.** Start in an upright kneeling position. Sit back onto your heels, then lean forward and rest your forehead on the floor, arms by your sides, palms facing up. Allow your body to relax completely as you breathe deeply in through your nose and out through your mouth. Feel your diaphragm rising and falling as air goes in and out of your body. Let your muscles sink deeper into the floor with each breath. Stay in this pose for 10 full breaths, or as long as you like. *Soothes your lower back; rejuvenates and nurtures your body.*

# CHAPTER FOUR

# The Supermodel Lower-Body Conditioner

## *. . . Starring Claudia Schiffer*

The first time I met Claudia Schiffer was at the Las Vegas warehouse of her boyfriend at the time, grand illusionist David Copperfield. Claudia was interested in making some exercise videos (as other supermodels have done), and she needed a fitness expert to help her design and choreograph the video workouts. I was one of a handful of personal trainers invited to audition for the job. After meeting with her producers, I flew to Vegas to interview with Claudia and her creative team.

When I arrived at David's warehouse, I thought I had the wrong address. The outside entryway was lined with mannequins in negligees—it looked like a lingerie shop! I rechecked the number on the front door. It matched the one I'd been given, but I still couldn't believe that I was in the right place. Then, out of the corner of my eye, I noticed a note pinned to one of the mannequins. It said, "Press my breast." It reminded me of something out of an X-rated *Scooby-Doo* cartoon. It was definitely the strangest doorbell I'd ever encountered.

Feeling like I was on an episode of *Candid Camera*, I went ahead and, well, pressed the breast. *Abracadabra*, a door opened and there was Claudia, looking every bit as gorgeous as she does in the *Sports Illustrated* swimsuit calendars. But instead of a bikini, she was wearing a cute T-shirt and exercise tights. She wasn't wearing any makeup, but she still looked stunning. As I stood face-to-face with her, I remember thinking, "Now I understand

> " Working with Kathy was an inspiration to me, and I hope an inspiration to all women. Her workout regimens are enjoyable and easy to follow, and her advice is honest. By simply taking time out to listen to our bodies, we can achieve realistic results on the inside as well as the outside. Exercise is incredibly important to women—it creates balance in our lives that combats the effects of natural and inevitable changes in our bodies. It is a tonic that can keep us young, give us strength, and improve our quality of life. "
>
> —Claudia Schiffer

## Workout Sneak Preview

Believe it or not, even supermodels like Claudia Schiffer need to work on firming those female trouble spots—especially the butt, hips, and thighs. Once a week, do this 20-minute targeted lower-body workout designed to get Claudia runway-ready, along with 25 minutes of fat-blasting cardio, and before you know it, you'll be smiling for the camera without covering up!

why some women are supermodels." She's a masterpiece—no wonder the world wants to look at her.

As it turned out, David's warehouse housed all of the props and materials used in his magic shows. Inside the building was everything that he needed to cut a woman in half, make his assistant—*poof!*—disappear, walk through the Great Wall of China, and fly through the air. It was also where he and his crew of helpers worked to develop new tricks. There were offices, a living room area with couches, a kitchen, a bedroom, and a full gym. But instead of trying to sneak a peek at the great master's "secrets," I focused on my job at hand.

After a tour of David's warehouse, Claudia and I sat down and talked about what she had in mind for her videos. We reviewed some exercise tapes made by other models to get an idea of the "competition" and, of course, how we could improve upon them. Claudia wanted her videos to be very sleek and stylized, with a cutting-edge "MTV look." From these initial conversations, I could tell that these wouldn't be your average exercise videos. They would be an artistic production of supermodel caliber.

About three days later, after I had returned to Los Angeles, Claudia's agent called and invited me to join the video team. I had passed the interview, and now it was time for me to put my training skills to the test. I was asked to return to Las Vegas and start working out with Claudia. Together, we needed to determine what kinds of moves to feature in the videos. I also needed to prepare her to do these exercises in front of a camera. At the time, I had no idea what she would be capable of physically.

For the next month, I flew back and forth from L.A. to Las Vegas on a daily basis. Every afternoon I drove to LAX, hopped on a plane, jumped in a cab, arrived at David's warehouse, and worked out with Claudia for about an hour. This gave us a chance to really get to know one another. Claudia was able to get a sense of what my technique was like and what the long-term results would be. At the same time, I learned what was important to her. She wanted her entire body to be stronger and more toned, especially her butt, thighs, abs, and arms.

It was at our first official training session that I asked Claudia to hold her body in a push-up position. I could see that her upper-body strength was, to be brutally honest, nonexistent. She couldn't do a single push-up. So I knew that upper-body conditioning would be a top priority. After we finished each workout, I would turn around and head back to Los Angeles. I certainly racked up a lot of frequent-flier miles, but it was worth it. Claudia and I developed a great chemistry and came up with some terrific ideas.

As we focused on Claudia's goals, we began to build the foundation for the fitness routines in the videos. We decided to do a series called *Perfectly Fit,* which would include four separate thirty-minute videos focusing on specific body parts: butt, legs, abs, and arms. The series was designed for quick, targeted training—something that Claudia, or anyone, could do anytime, anywhere.

And I mean *anywhere*! When David began his next tour, I became a tour-bus regular with Claudia. (She was an incredibly devoted girlfriend!) Let's just say that life on the road wasn't exactly glamorous. I slept on the bottom of a three-bed rack in the hallway of the bus. Every day, we'd arrive in a new city around 4 P.M., and David would set up for two or three hours. Meanwhile Claudia and I would search for a place in the building to work out. When his show started at around 7 or 8 P.M., Claudia's training sessions would begin.

While David was amazing his audience, I was amazed at how quickly Claudia was picking up the exercises. Usually we'd be in an empty room, exercising with nothing but a sturdy chair, a jump rope, a small ball, and free weights. These rooms were definitely better suited for board meetings than for getting a supermodel in shape for a breakout video series. But with some knowledge and creativity, you can get a fantastic workout no matter where you are.

Sometimes, before her training session, Claudia and I would go for a walk through town. It gave us a chance to explore a new city while stretching our legs and adding some cardio to her routine. Whenever possible, we would try to pick hilly streets to boost the intensity and increase the caloric burn. Walking uphill also happens to be a great workout for the butt and thighs.

While healthy eating on the road can be a challenge, Claudia was always careful to order wisely. If we were dining in a restaurant, she would ask for a salad or grilled fish or meat. At breakfast and lunch, she often asked for a fruit plate. She always ate her food in small portions, rather than stuffing herself with a large meal. She didn't have many vices, but she did love chocolate, as many of us do. As I explained earlier, it's important to make room in your diet for your favorite foods. Otherwise you're apt to feel deprived. But be sure to do so in moderation. For example, if you're craving a chocolate fix, take a small piece, eat it slowly, and savor every bite.

When we were finally ready to start shooting the videos, we were off jet-setting yet again. This time we headed to St. Barth's and Prague—two places I had never been before. St. Barth's is a tropical paradise in the French West Indies, with verdant hills, aquamarine water, and a gorgeous harbor lined with yachts and rustic fishing boats. It was so incredibly beautiful that, to this day, I long to return. We stayed in private bungalows that were part of a luxurious beachfront hotel. We'd certainly come a long way from David's tour bus!

## Semisweet News

When enjoyed in moderation, chocolate can be part of a healthy diet. It is a rich source of antioxidants called flavonoids, which have been shown to decrease the risk of cardiovascular disease and possibly cancer. Dark varieties, including bittersweet and semisweet, typically contain the most flavonoids. Just remember: Chocolate *is* high in fat and calories. One ounce of either dark, milk, or semisweet has approximately 140 to 150 calories and 8 to 10 grams of fat. So even if it offers health benefits, don't go overboard!

# Seared Tuna with Grilled Papaya, Cucumber, and Mint Vinaigrette

Over the past few years, we've learned the importance of including heart-healthy fish in our diets. One of my favorites is tuna, which is rich in omega-3 fatty acids, shown to reduce the risk of both heart disease and cancer. This healthy, Hawaiian-style recipe comes courtesy of my good friend Wolfgang Puck. He recommends searing the tuna on an outdoor or indoor grill, which you can also use to cook the papaya. You can find the special ingredients it calls for, as well as the tuna, in Asian markets and well-stocked supermarkets. **Makes 6 to 8 servings**

**Grilled Papaya, Cucumber, and Mint Vinaigrette**

½ strawberry papaya, seeded and peeled
1 teaspoon chili oil
Salt
½ cup red wine vinegar
¼ cup lime juice
2 tablespoons fish sauce (nuoc cham)
2 tablespoons soy sauce
⅓ cup peanut oil
¼ cup sesame oil
¼ to ½ cup diced Maui or red onion

¾ cup peeled, seeded, and diced cucumber
3 tablespoons chopped mint
1 tablespoon chopped fresh basil
1 teaspoon sugar
½ teaspoon white pepper

**Seared Tuna**

1½ pounds sushi-grade ahi tuna
Peanut oil
Salt
Freshly ground black pepper

1. Preheat a grill.

2. For the Grilled Papaya, Cucumber, and Mint Vinaigrette: Season the papaya half all over with chili oil and salt. Grill the papaya several minutes per side, just until it has grill marks and has begun to soften. Set it aside, leaving the grill hot. When the papaya is cool enough to handle, dice enough to measure ¾ cup. In a large nonreactive bowl, whisk together the vinegar, lime juice, fish sauce, and soy sauce. Whisk in the peanut oil and sesame oil. Add the papaya and onion and stir well. Add the cucumber, mint, basil, sugar, and white pepper, stir again, cover with plastic wrap, and refrigerate for 2 hours to let the flavors marry. The vinaigrette will keep for up to 24 hours in the refrigerator.

3. For the Seared Tuna: Drizzle the tuna with peanut oil and season with salt and black pepper. Place the tuna on the hot grill and sear it on each side just until the outside is browned and nicely marked with grill marks, 30 seconds to 1 minute per side; the inside should remain raw. Remove the tuna from the grill. Slice the tuna crosswise into ¼-inch-thick slices.

4. Arrange the slices overlapping on a serving platter or individual plates. Spoon the vinaigrette over and around the slices and serve immediately.

Every morning, I would open my sliding glass door and walk out onto the soft, warm sand. Since it wasn't tourist season, the island was quiet and peaceful. And the food was amazing. We would have colorful fruit salads for breakfast and fresh grilled mahimahi, salmon, sea bass, or swordfish for lunch and dinner. My mouth still waters just thinking about it. It's incredibly easy to eat healthfully when you have a variety of delicious, naturally slimming, and nutritious foods available as a matter of everyday course.

Prague was incredible, too, though totally different than St. Barth's. The capital of the Czech Republic, located in the heart of Eastern Europe, the city is filled with centuries-old bridges and cobblestone streets. It is home to ancient castles and towering churches with golden spires, which is why it is called the Hundred-Spired City. History and romance seem to follow you down every alleyway. Prague is a place that is close to Claudia's heart, as she had grown up in Germany. She wanted to share its beauty

## Does "Supermodel-Thin" Mean Fit?

Women who have battled weight gain over the years often jump to the conclusion that thin equals fit. They couldn't be more wrong. In fact, women who are skinny but out of shape are still at risk for a multitude of health problems, including heart attack, stroke, diabetes, and cancer. While excess pounds can contribute to these diseases, so can inactivity. Regardless of your weight, cardio exercise is crucial for a healthy heart and lungs. Strength training is also important for keeping your muscles and bones strong and staving off osteo-porosis. In fact, thin women are often at a higher-than-average risk of this condition, which can result in bone fractures. And all of us need to work on boosting flexibility and balance, especially as we age. This will help keep you active and mobile. So even if you're close to your ideal weight, or even supermodel slender, remember that regular physical activity is vital. It will help you improve your quality of life now, and maintain your freedom and independence in later years.

and majesty with other people. So we filmed part of each video on a rooftop overlooking the colorful city.

The videos turned out great, and Claudia's producers and friends couldn't believe the change in her physique. As I said earlier, the very first time I asked Claudia to do a push-up, she was barely able to do one. Now she could do three sets of fifteen. Her whole body not only looked strong, it actually was strong. Her butt and thighs were firmer, her stomach was flatter, and her arms were more defined. Claudia was in terrific shape, and it showed. People joked that David had waved his magic wand. But there was no magic involved. It was Claudia's hard work, combined with effective exercises to target each trouble area, that did the trick.

What follows is a condensed "best of" version of my training sessions with Claudia. This workout is designed to help you tone, tighten, lift, and strengthen your trouble zones, with an emphasis on the ones many of us sweat the most: our hips, buttocks, and thighs. It's easy, straightforward, and effective. Now say "Presto" three times, and you'll be ready to go!

# Claudia's Supermodel Lower-Body Conditioner

Do this workout once a week on Mondays. **For cardio:** You'll be doing a 25-minute, fat-blasting interval workout combining brisk walking and jumping rope. **For strength:** You'll do a 20-minute routine focusing on your buttocks, hips, thighs, and calves. This workout features some of my favorite classic strength exercises, as well as innovative moves requiring agility and balance.

You can do these cardio and strength workouts back-to-back or split them up between morning and evening.

### What You'll Need

- Watch with a timer
- Jump rope
- Sturdy chair
- Low (1 to 2 inches high) platform. (You can use anything that you can safely stand on, such as a step aerobics bench, two hardcover coffee table books, or a 2 × 4 piece of wood.)
- Dumbbell (3 to 5 pounds)
- Medium-sized ball (such as a basketball, soccer ball, volleyball, dodgeball, or small beach ball)

This interval workout combines brisk walking and jumping rope in order to blast calories and incinerate flab. Here's how it works: You'll do four minutes of walking followed by one minute of jumping rope, then repeat these intervals until you've walked a mile and a half. By alternating lower- and higher-intensity spurts of exercise, you can elevate your heart rate in a manageable way. This type of interval training allows you to boost your fitness level and burn more calories—without burning out.

Your goal should be to walk at a 15-minute-per-mile pace (or 4 miles per hour). The cardio portion of the workout should take about 25 to 30 minutes. (If you're walking slower than 15 minutes per mile, it could take slightly longer.)

If you haven't used a jump rope since grammar school, don't worry. Even if you weren't the double Dutch queen of your neighborhood, you'll just need a little practice to get the timing down. See Jump Rope Basics (page 72) for some tips on getting started. If you have chronic back pain or weak ankles, use an imaginary jump rope, march in place, or try another cardio activity such as climbing stairs or cycling instead. The goal is to get your heart rate up, so be sure to put some effort into it.

If you began the program by doing Michelle's Early Morning Start-up Workout, you may already have mapped out your walking route for this program. If not, start by getting in your car and using your odometer to measure a 1.5-mile path. (While you're doing this, you should also map out a 2-mile route, which you'll be using in the Charlie's Angels' Boot Camp Workout). Alternatively, you can walk on your local high school track (4 laps equal 1 mile). Or, if you can't do the workout outdoors, you can walk on a treadmill or even at your local shopping mall.

To get started, tie your jump rope around your waist. Wear a watch with a timer to keep track of your time. (A stopwatch will work, too.) Be sure to wear comfortable walking shoes or cross-trainers on your feet.

### Here's how the intervals break down

Minutes 1–4: Walk

Minute 5: Jump rope

Minutes 6–9: Walk

Minute 10: Jump rope

Minutes 11–14: Walk

Minute 15: Jump rope

Minutes 16–19: Walk

Minute 20: Jump rope

Minutes 21–25: Walk

**STRENGTH**

For maximum benefits and injury prevention, be sure your muscles are warm before starting this workout. (If you do these moves immediately following your cardio routine, you can skip the warm-up outlined below.) End each workout by doing the cool-down stretches on pages 85–87. Rest 15 to 60 seconds between exercises, depending on how you feel.

## Jump Rope Basics

I love teaching people to jump rope because I think it's one of the greatest exercises around. With a jump rope, you can blitz more than 100 calories in 10 minutes and boost your cardiovascular fitness. Best of all, it's fun! To get started, swing the rope with a smooth, rhythmic motion. Use your wrists to move the rope, not your shoulders, and keep your elbows close to your sides. Jump with your feet close to the floor to minimize impact. (You really only need to lift your feet an inch or so.) Continue increasing the speed of the rope as you become more comfortable with the motion. Take only one jump per revolution. If you miss at first, be patient and stick with it. In no time you'll be whipping the rope around and blasting calories like Sylvester Stallone in *Rocky*.

## Warm-up

Knee Lifts.  Stand with your feet hip-width apart, knees slightly bent, chest lifted, and belly button pulled in. Lift your right knee up toward your chest, then lower and repeat with left knee. Do this 10 times. Next, extend your arms in front of you at chest level, palms facing down. Lift your right knee and try to touch it to your right palm, then lower and repeat with left knee. Do this 10 times. Finally, lift your right knee up toward your chest and try to touch it to your left elbow. Lower and repeat with left knee and right elbow. Do this 10 times.

Repeat all 3 knee lifts (10 more times each), and you should be ready to start your workout.

## The Workout

**1. Power Chair Pose.**  Stand with your feet hip-width apart, chest lifted, and belly button pulled in. Contract your pelvic floor muscles, i.e., the muscles used to stop the flow of urine. Exhale as you bend your knees and lower your hips until your knees are bent at almost a 90-degree angle, simultaneously extending your arms up so they're next to your ears. Your torso should lean forward slightly. Relax your face, lift your chest, and point your tailbone toward the floor. It's as if you're sitting on an imaginary chair. Hold this position, inhaling and exhaling until you have taken 10 full breaths. Rest for 30 seconds. Repeat 4 times. *Targets quadriceps, hamstrings, buttocks, hips, back, shoulders, and core muscles, including the pubococcygeus (or PC) muscle.*

**2. a) Standing Rear Leg Lift.** Stand facing the back of a sturdy chair, about a foot away, with your chest lifted and belly button pulled in. Bend forward at your hips and rest your forearms on the chair back. Keeping your right knee slightly bent and belly button pulled in, exhale and squeeze your buttocks as you lift your left leg behind you as high as you can. Do this 10 times, then switch legs and repeat. *Targets buttocks and some hamstrings.*

**b) Calf Raise.**  Stand on your low platform—a stair, a step, a book, or a board—with your feet hip-width apart, chest lifted, and belly button pulled in. Your weight is on the balls of your feet and your heels are extending off the back edge of the platform. Lower your heels down a couple of inches, then rise up onto the balls of your feet and pause. Do this 15 times. When you're finished, bend your knees to loosen up your calves. *Targets calves.*

After you've completed both exercises, rest for 30 seconds, then repeat.

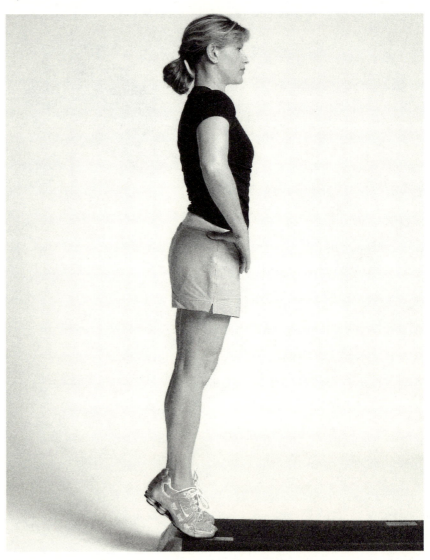

**3. Forward and Back Lunge.** Stand with your feet hip-width apart, arms by your sides, chest lifted, and belly button pulled in. Take a large step forward with your left foot. Exhale as you bend both knees into a lunge, so that your left knee is directly over your left ankle and your right knee points down to the floor, with the right heel lifted. Inhale, then exhale as you push back up with your left foot, straighten both your legs, and bring your feet back to starting position. Now, exhale as you take a large step backward with your left foot and bend your knees into another lunge. Your right knee is directly over your right ankle and your left knee points to the floor, with the left heel lifted. Inhale, then exhale as you push back to starting position. Repeat until you've done 8 forward and back lunges with your left leg. Switch legs and repeat. *Targets quadriceps, buttocks, hamstrings, inner and outer thighs.*

**4. One-Legged Squat.** *If this move seems too difficult, lower your hips just a few inches at first, then gradually progress to a full squat.* Stand with your arms by your sides, chest lifted, and belly button pulled in. With your right knee slightly bent, bring your left foot out in front of you. Keeping your back straight and your right knee directly in line with your toes, exhale as you bend your right knee and sit back as far as you can into a squat, simultaneously extending your arms at shoulder level. Breathe deeply as you hold for 2 counts. Exhale as you straighten your right knee and lower arms to return to starting position. Do this 8 to 10 times with your right leg, then switch legs and repeat. *Targets quadriceps, some hamstrings, buttocks.*

Repeat Exercises 1 through 4 again.

**5. Straight Weighted Leg Lift.** Lie on the floor on your left side, legs extended, hips stacked on top of each other, belly button pulled in. Your head, shoulders, and hips should form a straight line. Keeping your right leg straight and right foot flexed, bring your left knee in toward your chest, until it's in line with your hips. Place a 3- to 5-pound dumbbell on your right thigh and hold it there throughout the exercise. Exhale as you use your outer thigh muscles to slowly raise your right leg up about 12 inches, keeping your right kneecap facing forward. Don't raise your right leg too high or lean backward or forward with your torso. Lower your right foot back down to the floor. After doing this lift 15 times, take the weight off your leg and pull your right knee in toward your chest, then extend and straighten it, keeping your foot flexed. Do this 15 times. Switch legs and repeat. *Targets outer thighs.*

**6. Arm/Leg Opposition.**  Kneel on all fours, with your hands directly under your shoulders and your back flat. Keeping your belly button pulled in, exhale as you extend your left arm in front of you and your right leg behind you until they're both parallel to the floor. Breathe deeply as you hold for 30 seconds, continuing to keep your belly button pulled in. Lower to starting position, then repeat, this time extending your right arm and left leg. Continue alternating sides until you have done the move 2 times on each side. *Targets erector spinae, abdominals, buttocks, upper back.*

**7. Three-Side Ball Squeeze.** Lie on the floor on your left side, with your hips stacked on top of each other, belly button pulled in. Place your medium-sized ball between your knees, using your inner thigh muscles to hold the ball in place. Exhale as you press down with your top thigh and squeeze the ball 15 times. Keeping the ball between your knees, exhale as you roll onto your back and lift your toes up. Use both thighs to squeeze the ball 15 times. Finally, exhale as you roll over onto your right side and press down with your top thigh to squeeze the ball 15 times. *Targets inner thighs.*

**8. Hip Lift.** *I do this exercise with all of my female clients because it works the spot that everyone wants to tone—the area between your butt and the back of your thigh, or the bu-thigh, as Moon Zappa jokingly calls it.* Lie on your back in front of a chair, with your knees bent and your heels on the chair seat. (You can also use a coffee table instead of a chair.) Your knees should be directly above your hips, your arms by your sides. Exhale as you press your heels down into the chair seat and squeeze your buttocks until your hips lift off the floor. Pause, then lower your hips back down. Do this 10 times. Rest for 30 to 60 seconds, then repeat. *Targets buttocks.*

**9. One-Legged Bridge.** Lie on your back with your knees bent, your feet together and flat on the floor, and your arms by your sides. Keeping your belly button pulled in and your knees together, exhale and extend your left leg straight in front of you as you lift your hips and back up off the floor into a modified "bridge." Your upper arms, shoulders, neck, and head stay on the floor. Your hips should be square, not tilted. Squeeze your inner thighs and keep your knees together to avoid dropping your left hip. Breathe deeply as you hold for 15 to 30 seconds. Lower to starting position. Repeat, extending your right leg. *Targets buttocks.*

**10. Side-Lying Body Lift.** Lie on your left side with your legs extended, supporting your body weight on your left elbow and left hip. For balance, your right leg can be slightly in front of your right leg. Rest your right arm on the side of your body. Keeping your belly button pulled in, exhale as you lift your hips up until your body forms a straight line from head to toe. You will be using your upper hip muscles, glutes, and abs. Hold for 5 counts, then lower your hips back to the starting position. Do this 2 times, then switch sides and repeat. *Targets core muscles (abs and lower back) and outer hips; your shoulders work as stabilizers.*

Repeat exercises 6 through 10 again.

## Cool-Down Stretches

**Cat Stretch.** Kneel on all fours, with your hands directly under your shoulders and your knees in line with your hips. Keeping your belly button pulled in, exhale as you round your back up like a cat, dropping your head toward the floor. Breathe deeply as you hold this position for 2 or 3 counts, then return to starting position. Repeat 5 times, or as many times as you like. *Stretches upper back, lower back, shoulders.*

**Downward Dog.** Kneeling on all fours, exhale as you press your hands into the floor and straighten your legs to lift your hips up toward the ceiling. With your belly button pulled in, continue lifting your tailbone up as you press your heels down to the floor as far as you comfortably can. Your body should look like an inverted V. Breathe deeply as you hold for 30 seconds, or as long as you comfortably can, then return to starting position. *Stretches hamstrings, calves, Achilles tendons, upper back.*

**Hip Flexor/Thigh Stretch.** From an upright kneeling position, place your right foot on the floor in front of you, with your right knee bent and in line with your toes. Your hands should be on your hips or, if you're flexible enough, you can place them on the floor on either side of your right foot. Press forward with your hips to stretch the front of your left thigh. Breathe deeply as you hold for 30 seconds, or as long as you can. Switch legs and repeat. *Stretches hip flexors and quadriceps.*

**Child's Pose.**  Start in an upright kneeling position. Sit back onto your heels, then lean forward and rest your forehead on the floor, arms by your sides, palms facing up. Allow your body to relax completely as you breathe deeply, in through your nose and out through your mouth. Feel your diaphragm rising and falling as air goes in and out of your body. Let your muscles sink deeper into the floor with each breath. Stay in this pose for 10 full breaths, or as long as you like. *Soothes your lower back; rejuvenates and nurtures your body.*

## Spicy Pineapple, Apricot, and Jicama Salsa

For this salsa, chef Hollis Wilder uses an unexpected combination of sweet and spicy ingredients. It's delicious with low-fat tortilla chips, or as a zesty topping for fish, chicken, or any other poultry.

**Makes 1½ cups**

¼ small ripe pineapple, peeled and diced in ¼-inch pieces
½ cup jicama, peeled and diced into ¼-inch pieces
⅓ cup dried apricots, coarsely chopped

¼ small red onion, chopped
½ bunch fresh cilantro, finely chopped
½ fresh habanero or Scotch bonnet chile, finely chopped

In a bowl, combine all ingredients and season with salt. Salsa may be made up to 6 hours ahead. Keep covered and chilled.

# CHAPTER FIVE

# Rachel's Super-Sexy Upper Body–Sculpting Workout

## . . . Starring Jennifer Aniston

*I* begin training Jennifer Aniston right around the time that *Friends* debuted, in the fall of 1994. The show was already getting a buzz, so I knew who she was. But it wasn't until a year or so later, when *Friends* achieved megahit status, that she truly became a household name. Little did I know that this funny, down-to-earth, twenty-five-year-old actress would end up single-handedly revolutionizing women's hairstyles, taking home a million-dollar-per-episode paycheck, and marrying one of the sexiest men on earth, Brad Pitt.

When Jennifer and I first met, she wasn't nearly as lean and buff as she is today. She had dropped some weight since starring in the TV version of *Ferris Bueller's Day Off* several years earlier, but still had a kind of youthful, just-out-of-college look. By Hollywood standards, she may not have been thin enough, but she certainly wasn't overweight. As Jennifer was once quoted as saying, "I wasn't fat, I was Greek—and Greeks are round, with big asses and boobs."

Jennifer and I worked out two or three times a week either at her home, at a private gym in West Hollywood called Muscle Under, or at the Warner Brothers studio where *Friends* was filmed. At Warner Brothers, I would often see other celebrities shaping up between takes. One day, Brooke Shields was right next to us doing biceps curls—this was during her *Suddenly*

" I was working out with Kathy right after *Friends* started its run. She taught me that basic exercises like walking, stretching, and using my own body weight for resistance will get me into the best physical condition. When I am able to exercise, I always feel good about myself and am much more likely to stick to a healthy lifestyle. "

—Jennifer Aniston

## Workout Sneak Preview

In less than the time it takes to watch an episode of *Friends,* you can finish this upper-body workout featuring some of the exercises I did with America's favorite friend, Jennifer Aniston. With this 25-minute series of weight-lifting moves, many of which are performed on top of a stability ball, you can tone your arms, shoulders, back, and chest muscles. Not only will you see more definition when you sport sexy tops, you'll enhance your posture and have an easier time doing everyday tasks such as carrying grocery bags or picking up your kids.

*Susan* days. I hadn't seen her since the time she had been a surprise guest at one of my training sessions at the Zappas!

The first time I went to Jennifer's Hollywood home, I was impressed by its unassuming quality. It was relatively small and modest, decorated in a very bohemian style with lots of color. The house was situated on the side of a mountain, with sweeping views of the Los Angeles basin. Jennifer had turned one of her spare bedrooms into an office/workout room, where she had a treadmill and dumbbells. (Later she added an elliptical machine, a weight bench, and an exercise step.) Not to sound cliché, but she really was so nice and girlfriend-like. She immediately made me feel comfortable and was incredibly easy to talk to. Plus, as you might have guessed from watching her on *Friends,* she has a great sense of humor.

During our workouts, Jennifer typically wore thin sweats with a tank top. She pulled her soon-to-be-world-famous "Rachel" haircut back into a ponytail and always sported the hottest Nikes. In fact, she turned me on

## Feng Shui Fitness

While I can't say I'm a follower of feng shui, I believe that an inviting workout environment can do wonders for your energy levels and motivation. Face it, if your exercise bike is in a dark, dank corner of your basement, are you really going to want to go down there and use it? Probably not. But if you create a warm and appealing space for working out, you'll be more likely to follow through. Try decorating your walls with inspirational prints and colors that invigorate you. For some of you it might be music and entertainment that will keep you pumped for your daily workouts. If so, try placing a small TV or CD player in the room. Keep your favorite CDs nearby or make a CD of your favorite dance tunes. Or take Sarah Jessica Parker's "scentsational" advice. One of my former clients, she places scented candles and incense in her workout area to keep her moving, choosing fragrances that boost her energy and mood. (Her husband, actor Matthew Broderick, has said that one of the things he loves about Sarah Jessica is that she always makes things smell so great!) We're all different, so figure out what works for you. Once you shape up your space, you should start looking forward to your workouts instead of finding excuses to skip them!

to a cool new shoe called the Nike Air Rift, which has a stylish Velcro closure and a split toe. Jennifer's Air Rifts were black and red, but they come in other colors. I love them so much that I currently have three pairs in my closet! When I wear them around town, I feel as hip as any television star, and I always get a lot of appreciative looks and compliments.

As for fitness goals, Jennifer wanted to get leaner and in better overall shape. While she was fairly strong, she needed to be more consistent with her workouts. Like many people, she tended to do the same activities all the time. My job was to shake her out of her fitness rut and encourage her to push her body a little harder. Jennifer certainly didn't need me to motivate her, but she did need some inspiration and guidance. No matter what I had in store for her, she was energetic and ready to go. At the end of each training session, she was always eager to schedule the next one.

As Jennifer got stronger and fitter, she started to look really sculpted, and suddenly it seemed like everyone was talking about her body. (To this day, I'm asked about it all the time. And I mean *all the time*!) Her upper body, in particular, became the envy of women everywhere. They wanted to know how she got those sexy toned arms and shapely shoulders. One of the reasons her upper body gets so much attention is that she is always sporting sleeveless tops and dresses. Just look at past episodes of *Friends* or paparazzi photographs of her at the latest Hollywood hot spot!

While consistent workouts contributed significantly to Jennifer's physical transformation, dietary changes also played a major role. When I met her, she had been seeing a registered dietician to learn more about nutrition. Not long after that, she began following The Zone, a diet developed by Dr. Barry Sears that is based on controlling the hormone insulin. The goal is to keep your insulin level in a particular "zone"—not too high and not too low—throughout the day. You do this by balancing your intake of protein and carbohydrates, which have a dramatic impact on insulin production. To stay in the zone, you must also eat every four to five hours throughout the day, whether or not you're hungry.

Though I don't endorse diets like these, I know a few friends and clients, including Jennifer and Cindy Crawford, who have tried The Zone and loved the results. But I must warn you that not everyone has success

## Perfectly Poached Shrimp with Green Goddess Sauce

Hollis Wilder whips together this tasty meal for Debra Messing, Megan Mullally, and the other goddesses on her *Will & Grace* set. It's a low-fat, flavor-packed favorite, with a heavenly combination of herbs and spices. Best of all, since it's served cold, it can be prepared ahead and stored in the refrigerator in an air-tight container.

**Makes 4 servings**

1 small garlic clove
½ cup low-fat or nonfat mayonnaise
½ cup packed fresh parsley, chopped
⅓ cup fresh chives, chopped
⅓ cup green onions (white and pale green parts only), chopped
1½ tablespoons fresh tarragon, chopped
1 canned anchovy fillet

1 teaspoon rice vinegar
Salt and pepper

1 tablespoon Kosher salt
1 pound uncooked, unpeeled jumbo shrimp (about 20)
Freshly ground pepper to taste

**For the sauce:** Finely chop garlic in food processor. Add mayonnaise, parsley, chives, onions, tarragon, anchovy, and vinegar; blend until smooth and pale green. Season sauce to taste with salt and pepper. Transfer sauce to serving bowl. Cover and refrigerate until cold. (Can be prepared 2 days ahead. Keep refrigerated.)

**For the shrimp:** Fill 2 large bowls with ice water; set aside. Bring extra large pot of water to boil over high heat. Add ½ tablespoon Kosher salt to boiling water; return to a boil. In another large bowl, rub shrimp with remaining half tablespoon of salt. Add shrimp to boiling water until just cooked through, about 3 minutes (water will not return to boil). Immediately drain shrimp in colander, then quickly divide between prepared bowls of ice water; cool completely. Drain well. Peel and devein shrimp, leaving tails intact. Arrange shrimp on platter. (Can be prepared 4 days ahead. Keep refrigerated.) Serve shrimp with sauce.

with this kind of eating plan. While people do seem to shed pounds on The Zone and other popular diets, it takes dedication and diligence. The guidelines are quite rigid, making them difficult to adhere to in the long run. As a result, many people end up returning to their old eating habits and gaining weight again. I'm not trying to talk you out of trying a plan that might work for you. But before signing up, be aware of the potential drawbacks. Don't forget: In order to make permanent changes, you need a smart diet and exercise plan that you can maintain for a lifetime.

Over the years, Jennifer has been able to uphold her commitment to eating right, and it shows. If you ask me, she's a perfect example of how you can change your body with regular exercise and a healthy diet. But she wouldn't have been successful if she had altered her habits for a few weeks or months, then stopped. There simply are no quick fixes. Also, changes don't happen overnight, so Jennifer had to be patient. She stayed focused on improving her strength and fitness, rather than her appearance. The end result was that she lost body fat while gaining muscle, creating that lean, toned, highly sculpted look that she has today.

As for those much-talked-about arms, the exercises in Rachel's Super-Sexy Upper Body–Sculpting Workout are one key part of the equation. By doing these moves once a week, as part of your weekly exercise plan, you can hit all the important spots on your upper body. You'll sculpt and define the front of your arms, while getting rid of the jiggle on the back of your arms (or the "flesh flags," as Katie Couric calls them). Your shoulders will become stronger and more shapely, which will also help to visually reduce the size of your waist. You'll also strengthen your chest and upper back muscles, so you'll look extra-sexy in a low-cut shirt or backless dress.

This upper-body workout features traditional strength moves using either dumbbells or only your body weight for resistance. You'll be performing many of these exercises on a stability ball. When you work on an unstable surface you're forced to use small, stabilizing muscles throughout your body to stay balanced. In particular, you'll need to engage your core muscles, which are so important for good balance and beautiful posture. Don't forget: When you stand tall, your body looks better. And when you look better, you feel better about yourself.

## Excuses, excuses!

The most common excuse for not exercising is "I don't have enough time!" But consider this: There are 168 hours in one week. If you get 8 hours of sleep a night and spend 40 hours working each week, you still have 72 hours for everything else!

Squeezing in 30 to 60 minutes of exercise each day will only use about 4 to 8 hours of your free time. Sounds like a small investment for a lifetime of healthy returns. Wouldn't you agree?

I've used these exercises with Jennifer as well as other sitcom stars, including *Married with Children*'s Katey Sagal and Christina Applegate, Queen Latifah (during her *Livin' Single* days), and *Becker*'s Nancy Travis, and with actresses Jamie Gertz and Candice Bergen. You can do this 25-minute routine while watching your favorite Tuesday-night sitcom—or one of those *Friends* reruns on cable! Let's be honest, most of us watch at least one 30-minute show each week. So why not turn your guilty pleasure into your guiltless treasure by doing these moves while you watch them? This way, they will fit into your life effortlessly and be more likely to stick!

# Rachel's Super-Sexy Upper Body–Sculpting Workout

D o this workout once a week on Tuesdays. For fast, visible results, you'll be using a time-effective technique called "super-
setting"—doing back-to-back exercises to target different
muscle groups, with no rest in between. For example, you'll
do a biceps curl (to strengthen the front of your arms) immediately followed by an overhead press (to work your shoulders). Because you keep
moving (instead of resting between sets), your heart rate stays elevated
for a bigger caloric burn.

Before getting started, take a few minutes to practice balancing your
body on top of the stability ball. Sit on the center of the ball with your
knees bent, feet shoulder-width apart, arms by your sides. Keep your
chest lifted and belly button pulled in. Your spine should be in a natural
position; don't arch your back. Once you find your balance, it should be
easy to remain stable as you do the exercises.

## What You'll Need

- Stability ball
- Dumbbells (You'll be using both "light" and "heavy" weights in
  this workout. If you're new to strength training, use 3-pound
  dumbbells as your light weights and 5-pound dumbbells as your
  heavy weights. If you've been doing some form of strength
  training, use 5-pound dumbbells as your light weights and
  8-pound dumbbells as your heavy weights. If your muscles don't
  feel challenged by the final few repetitions, switch to heavier
  weights as long as you can maintain proper form.)

- Sturdy chair
- Towel or exercise mat (optional)

## Warm-up

Hula Dancing on Ball.  Sit on top of the ball with your knees bent, feet flat on the floor, chest lifted, and belly button pulled in. Place your hands on your hips. Breathe deeply as you slowly swing your hips from side to side. Do this 10 times. Next, rock your hips forward and back. Do this 10 times.

**Seated Ball Walk.** Sitting upright on the ball, exhale as you walk your feet forward so that the ball rolls up your back, keeping your belly button pulled in. Continue until your upper back, neck, and shoulders are fully supported on the ball. Pause, then curl your torso slightly forward and walk your feet back to return to an upright seated position. Do this 5 times.

**Overhead Reach on Ball.** Sitting upright on the ball, exhale as you extend both arms straight up overhead. Breathe deeply as you reach your arms toward the ceiling. Hold for 5 counts. Next, alternate arms, reaching up with your left for one count, then with your right. Continue alternating for 20 counts.

After you have finished all three moves, you should be ready to start your workout.

## The Workout

**1. a) Biceps Curl on Ball.** Holding a heavy weight in each hand, sit upright on the ball with your arms by your sides, palms facing in. Keep your chest lifted and belly button pulled in. Exhale as you slowly bend your elbows to curl the weights up toward your shoulders, simultaneously rotating your forearms so that your palms face up at the top of the lift. Inhale as you slowly lower the weights back down to starting position, turning your palms in. Do this 8 to 10 times, then immediately start the next exercise. *Targets biceps (front of arm) and core muscles (abs and lower back).*

**b) Rear Raise-up on Ball.** *You may be able to do this exercise with your heavy weights. If it's too difficult, switch to your light weights.* Holding your heavy weights, sit upright on the ball with your arms by your sides, palms facing in. Keep your chest lifted and belly button pulled in. Keeping your arms straight and close to your sides, exhale as you lift them back and up behind you as high as you can, bending forward slightly at your hips. Pause, then slowly lower your arms to starting position. Do this 8 times. *Targets rear shoulders, triceps (back of arm), core muscles.*

After you've completed both exercises, rest for 30 seconds, then repeat the superset.

**2. a) One-Legged Lateral Raise.** Holding your light weights, stand with your arms by your sides, palms facing in, chest lifted, belly button pulled in. Keeping your right knee slightly bent and your torso upright, exhale as you lift your left knee up as high as you can, without leaning forward or back. Hold this position by pulling your belly button in toward your spine. Keeping your elbows slightly bent, exhale as you slowly raise your arms directly out to your sides up to shoulder height, so your body forms a T. Don't lock your elbows at the top of the lift. Inhale as you slowly lower your arms back down to starting position, keeping your left knee lifted. Do this 10 times, then immediately start the next exercise. *Targets middle shoulders, core muscles.*

**b) One-Legged Front Raise.** Still holding your light weights, switch legs so you're balancing on your left leg and your right knee is lifted. Your arms are by your sides, palms facing in, and your chest is lifted, belly button pulled in. Keeping your elbows slightly bent, exhale as you slowly lift the weights straight out in front of you to shoulder height. Inhale as you slowly lower the weights to starting position. Do this 10 times. *Targets front and back shoulders, core muscles.*

After you've completed both exercises, rest for 30 seconds, then repeat the superset.

**3. a) Punching Bag on Ball.** Sit upright on the ball with your arms by your sides, palms facing in. Keep your chest lifted and belly button pulled in. Visualize a punching bag in front of you. Exhale as you do a cross punch into the imaginary bag with your right fist. Inhale as you return to starting position, then exhale and pull your right arm back as you do a cross punch with your left fist. Continue in a rhythmic fashion, one punch after the next. Do this 20 times (10 punches with each hand), then immediately start the next exercise. *Targets core muscles and some shoulder.*

**b) Chest Press on Ball.** Holding your heavy weights, sit upright on the ball, then walk your feet forward until you're in a supine position, with shoulders and head supported on the ball. Lift up your hips so that your body looks like a table. Squeeze your buttocks together and pull your belly button in toward your spine. Bend your arms up and rest your weights on your shoulders. Keeping your wrists straight, exhale as you press the weights up directly above your shoulders, until your arms are straight but not locked. Slowly lower the weights back down to starting position. Do this 10 times. When you're done, walk back up to an upright seated position holding the weights by your shoulders. Or, to make it easier, put the weights down on the floor one at a time before returning to the upright seated position. *Targets chest, front shoulders, core muscles.*

After you've completed both exercises, rest for 30 seconds, then repeat the superset.

**4. Kneeling Triceps Extension.** Holding a light weight in your right hand, stand facing a sturdy chair with your right leg slightly to the right of it. Place your left knee and left hand on the chair seat, then lean forward so that your back is flat. (You may need to move your right foot out to the side in order to achieve a flat back.) Keeping your belly button pulled in, raise your right elbow up and back until your upper arm is almost parallel to the floor. Now, exhale as you straighten your right arm, using the muscle in the back of your upper arm to lift the weight up and back. Inhale as you bend your right arm to lower the weight to starting position, without moving your upper arm. Do this 10 times. Rest for 30 seconds, then repeat with the same arm. Switch arms and repeat. *Targets triceps.*

**5. Kneeling One-Arm Row.** Start in the same position as the Kneeling Triceps Extension, holding a heavy weight in your right hand. Let your right arm hang by your right side. Exhale as you bend your right elbow to raise the weight up toward your underarm, lifting until your elbow is slightly higher than your back. Keep your elbow close to your torso and pointing directly behind you. The motion is a bit like starting a lawnmower. Pause, then inhale as you slowly lower the weight to starting position. Do this 10 times. Take a break, then repeat with the same arm. Switch arms and repeat. *Targets middle back, upper back, rear shoulders.*

**6. Bent-Knee Push-up Pulse.** From a kneeling position, lean forward and place your hands on the floor slightly wider than shoulder-width apart, arms and knees supporting your body. Squeeze your abs and buttocks to form a straight line from head to knees. Keeping your back straight and belly button pulled in, exhale as you slowly bend your arms to lower your chest until your upper arms are parallel to the floor (this should take 2 counts). Pulse up and down slightly (like a mini push-up) for 4 counts. Use your chest and upper arm muscles to push back up to bent-knee push-up position (this should take 2 counts). Repeat 3 times. If you can't do the pulses, do 8 traditional push-ups and try to hold for 1 pulse each time. *Targets chest, shoulders, triceps, core muscles.*

**7. a) Table.** Sit on the floor with your knees bent, feet hip-width apart, hands behind you on the floor, fingers pointing toward you. Keeping your belly button pulled in, exhale as you press up with your hips until your torso is parallel to the floor, like a tabletop. Keep your neck relaxed, but don't let it drop down. Imagine having a martini glass on the center of your belly—don't let it spill! Breathe deeply as you hold for 15 seconds. *Targets core muscles, triceps, buttocks, shoulders.*

**b) T Pose.** Roll onto your left side and extend your legs straight, feet stacked on top of each other. Lift your head and shoulders and place your left hand directly below your shoulder. Lift your hips to form a straight line from your head to your feet. Exhale as you extend your right arm straight up so that your body looks like a T. Breathe deeply as you hold for 15 to 30 seconds, or as long as you can, while maintaining good form. *Targets core muscles, hips, upper back, arms, shoulders.*

After you've completed both exercises, rest for 30 seconds, then repeat the superset, this time doing the T Pose on your right side. End by doing the Table one more time, if desired.

**8. Reverse Fly on Ball.** Put your light weights on the floor next to the stability ball. Kneel in front of the ball and lean forward onto it, rolling forward a little so that your belly is supported on top of the ball and your legs are straight, with your weight resting on your toes. Your body should form a straight line from head to heels. Now, grasp a dumbbell in each hand, allowing the weights to rest on the floor. Keeping your back straight and elbows slightly bent, exhale and squeeze your shoulder blades together as you lift the weights up and out to the sides, to slightly higher than shoulder level. Inhale and relax your shoulder blades as you lower the weights to starting position. Do this 10 times. Rest for 30 seconds, then repeat. *Targets rear shoulders, upper back, core muscles.*

**9. Concentration Curl on Ball.** Holding a heavy weight in your right hand, sit upright on the ball with your legs more than shoulder-width apart. Keeping your back straight and your belly button pulled in, lean forward and rest your right elbow on the inside of your right thigh, then straighten your right arm to lower the weight toward the floor. Exhale as you slowly curl the weight up toward your right shoulder, keeping your wrist straight. Pause, then inhale as you lower to starting position. Do 2 sets of 10 with your right arm, then switch sides and repeat. *Targets biceps and core muscles.*

**10. Shoulder Shrugs.** Holding your heavy weights, stand with your feet together, chest lifted, belly button pulled in, arms by your sides. Pull your shoulders back and down as far as they naturally go. Keeping your back straight, exhale as you slowly shrug your shoulders to your ears. Inhale as you slowly lower to starting position. Keep the movement very controlled. Do this 8 times. *Targets shoulders.*

## Cool-Down Stretches

**Shoulder Release.** From an upright standing position, interlink your fingers in front of you, then flip your hands so your palms are facing down. Exhale as you lift your arms above your head, palms facing up to the ceiling, and stretch up as far as you comfortably can. Breathe deeply as you hold for 30 seconds. Inhale as you lower to starting position. Do this 3 or 4 times. *Stretches shoulders.*

**Posture Clasp.** Kneel on the floor, then reach back with your left arm and place your left hand on the middle of your back, palm facing out. Exhale as you extend your right arm overhead, then bend your elbow and reach your right hand down your back toward your left hand. Try to clasp your fingers or touch your hands. Breathe deeply as you hold for 30 seconds. Switch arms and repeat. *Stretches triceps, front and back shoulders, chest.*

**Reverse Prayer.** Kneeling on the floor, reach around with your hands and place them in a prayer position against your back, keeping your chest lifted and belly button pulled in. Breathe deeply as you hold for 30 seconds. Release, then repeat. *Stretches shoulders and chest; encourages good posture.*

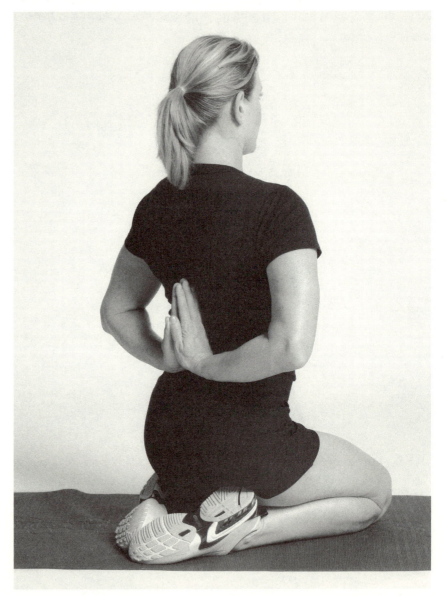

**Extended Child's Pose.** From an upright kneeling position, sit back onto your heels, then lean forward and rest your forehead on the floor, arms extended straight out in front of you. Allow your body to relax completely as you breathe deeply in through your nose and out through your mouth. Feel your diaphragm rising and falling as air goes in and out of your body. Let your muscles sink deeper into the floor with each breath. Stay in this pose for 10 full breaths, or as long as you like. *Soothes your lower back; rejuvenates and nurtures your body.*

## Mock Guac

I love guacamole! Thanks to Hollis Wilder, one of my favorite indulgences has gotten a healthy makeover. Enjoy her Mock Guac with veggie sticks or pita bread triangles for a low-fat, flavor-packed snack.  **Makes about 4 servings**

- 1 10-ounce package frozen peas
- 1 tablespoon flax oil
- 1 to 2 teaspoons ground cumin
- 1 teaspoon lemon juice
- ½ teaspoon salt
- Pepper
- A few shakes of Tabasco sauce
- 1 to 2 tablespoons water

Put all of the ingredients in a blender and process until smooth. If the consistency isn't right, add more water. Adjust the seasoning to taste.

# 6

# The Hidden Hills Workout
## . . . Starring My Neighbors and Me!

" Before I joined Kathy's Hidden Hills class, I'd never been one to work out. I'd been slender my entire life, and assumed that the only reason to exercise was to lose weight. Then I hit my forties, and my body started to change. Even though I was eating very little, I was putting on weight, and I had no energy or stamina. I went to Kathy's class one morning and I thought I was going to die! The cardio was so hard for me, and I had absolutely no upper-body strength. I forced myself to go back every day. Now, several years later, exercise is a very important part of my life, as natural as brushing my teeth. Kathy isn't in this to make us look twenty again. It's about having a healthy body and self-image. What's amazing is that, at age forty-nine, I'm now in better shape and health than I have ever been. I have endurance that I never thought possible, as well as a lot more energy and better balance. "

—Belle Schwartz, Hidden Hills workout group member

*I* live in Hidden Hills, an old ranching community in the western foothills of the San Fernando Valley, about forty-five minutes northwest of downtown Los Angeles and fifteen minutes northeast of Malibu. It's a small country town where you're as likely to see a white mare crossing the street as a kindergartner on his way to school. Seriously, if you were to casually stroll through the neighborhood that I call home, you'd have no idea that you were in Los Angeles County. That's one of the reasons Billy and I love it so much.

As you pull into town, you're met by a rustic white arch that says HIDDEN HILLS. There are about 650 homes located in our town, which is slightly less than two square miles in size. There are no sidewalks or streetlights, and not a single traffic signal. Almost every ranch-style house is surrounded by a white wooden fence, and many residents have horses, corrals, and barns in their backyards.

This lovely rural area is a wonderful place to raise a family, which is one of the main reasons that we live here. My eight-year-old twins attend the local school, which is only half a mile from our house. Since my four-year-old son is still at home, I, along with some other neighborhood moms, take turns hosting "Mommy and Me" classes for our little ones. Our dogs have the run of the backyard, and someday my husband and I hope to purchase a horse or two to join the others in the community.

But there's more to Hidden Hills than white fences, horses, and celebrities. (Did I mention that Will and Jada Pinkett Smith, Dr. Laura

" Two things come to mind immediately when I think of the benefits of working out with Kathy. First is that no matter how challenging her class is, I *always* feel better afterward! Second, I know that she cares deeply about what I'm doing, and how I'm doing, because she understands the benefits. It's not about what is happening externally, it's all about how healthy I am internally. Because the bottom line is, 'If you feel good, you look good, darling!' "

—Nathalie Blossom, Hidden Hills workout group member

## Workout Sneak Preview

This 25-minute strength and cardio circuit is based on the fun weekly classes that I teach at my local community center in the Los Angeles suburb of Hidden Hills. It's an energizing, calorie-blasting workout that's designed to build endurance, strength, coordination, balance, and flexibility. With this routine, you'll definitely feel your heart pumping and work up a sweat!

Schlessinger, David Bryan, a.k.a. Sinbad, actor/pro wrestler Dwayne "The Rock" Johnson, comedian Howie Mandel, drummer Alex Van Halen, and Tae Bo creator Billy Blanks all live nearby?) When I look around, I see a fabulous place for working out and getting fit. It's truly an outdoors lover's paradise, with beautiful rolling hills and acres of hiking and equestrian trails connected to every property.

After moving to Hidden Hills almost four years ago, I started teaching a fitness class at our local community center about three days a week. I thought it would be a great way to get to know my new neighbors and help all of us stay in shape. To spread the word, I made a flyer and called some of my neighbors and other local women I knew. They called their friends, and it took off from there. Since we were operating on a next-to-nothing budget, everyone started going to garage sales to look for equipment, such as jump ropes, exercise steps, and mats, to use in our classes.

On a typical week, there will be anywhere from two to twelve women, ranging in age from their twenties to their sixties, in each class. With the exception of Julia Roberts, who occasionally makes a guest appearance,

## Lime-Soy Vinaigrette

This zesty salad dressing from Hollywood nutrition guru Carrie Wiatt is deliciously light. Each two-tablespoon serving has only 20 calories and 1 gram of fat. I like to make a batch on Sunday and keep it in a refrigerated jar for easy access during the week. For a quick and tasty lunch, buy a bag of prewashed greens or spinach. Add sliced carrots, mushrooms, tomatoes, or your favorite veggies, and top with a dash of vinaigrette and a sprinkle of walnuts. For protein, top with slices of grilled chicken or tuna.

**Makes 2 cups**
**Serving Size: 2 tablespoons**

⅜ cup rice vinegar
⅛ cup low-sodium soy sauce
1½ teaspoons dark sesame oil
⅛ cup fresh lime juice

¾ teaspoon lemon zest
¾ teaspoon fresh ginger root, minced
1½ cloves garlic, minced

In a small mixing bowl, whisk together all ingredients. Use immediately, or cover and refrigerate up to 1 week. Return to room temperature and stir to blend before using.

## The Kathy Kaehler Hill Challenge

If you live in a hilly place, take advantage of it! Walking or jogging uphill is a great way to incinerate calories while seriously sculpting your lower-body muscles. Check your watch and time each trip from the bottom to the top—and vice-versa. Next time you see that hill or a similar one, do it again and try to beat your previous time. It's also a fun game to play with a partner—it can spur some natural competition, helping to improve both your fitness level and physique.

these women aren't celebrities dealing with film schedules and modeling shoots. They're regular people leading regular lives, busy trying to earn livings, raise children, and maintain homes.

During our hour-long classes, we either do cardio or strength training, or a combination of both. On those beautiful, sunny Southern California mornings, we sometimes venture outside for a run/walk in the hills. One of my favorite places to go is Saddle Creek Road, a seriously steep hill that seems to go straight up.

Sometimes I begin class by leading everyone on a group walk up Saddle Creek to get our blood moving and hearts pumping. It's an incredible warmup. When I have a new recruit in class, she's usually certain that she's going to drop dead before reaching the halfway mark. But after a few weeks, this very same woman can make it up the entire hill without getting winded. That's what I call progress!

After taking her first Hidden Hills class, one mother in her mid-forties was shocked to discover how weak she was, especially her upper body. She'd been walking to maintain her weight, but she hadn't done any formal exercise for a long time. She couldn't even hold herself in a push-up position. I could see that she was feeling discouraged, so I promised that we would work on it gradually. Each class, she'd do a little more. If she stuck with it, I told her that she'd be amazed at what she could do. Sure enough, three months later, she was able to do three sets of eight push-ups. A lot of people would have given up, but she didn't. And now it really shows. She's more positive and confident, and her arms look much more defined.

## Family Fitness

As mothers and caregivers, we often put our family's needs ahead of our own. But by neglecting your body, you not only do a disservice to yourself—your family will suffer, too. Staying healthy and fit will allow you to be a better mom, daughter, sister, or wife. You'll have more energy and be in a better mood. And by taking care of yourself, you can make sure that you're still around when your children graduate from college, walk down the aisle, and start a family of their own.

But the question is, how do you find time for exercise when you have children who need you? It's easy: Get active with your kids. Combining family and workout time can be rewarding on numerous levels. Maybe you can share your love of a favorite sport with your kids. Or maybe you'll all just laugh and enjoy each other's company as you take a bike ride around your neighborhood. Regardless of the activity, your children will learn by example. If they see you heading out for a walk or a tennis match, or sweaty and glowing after a great workout, chances are they'll be inspired.

By encouraging me to be active as a child, my parents helped instill a love of movement in me and taught me the benefits of exercise. Today, Billy and I are trying to do the same for our three young boys. We want our sons to understand that exercise is something that our bodies need. We constantly try to reinforce how being strong and flexible will help them improve their lives. Every day I ask them, "What did you do for your body today?"

Incorporating a similar philosophy into your family life will benefit your children as well as yourself. If you're trying to set a good example for your kids, you just may avoid the temptation to skip a workout—and teach them a valuable lesson about the importance of fitness.

When you learn to rock climb or scuba dive, one of the first things you're taught is the buddy system: never climb or dive without a partner. If you ask me, the buddy system isn't just for extreme sports. While working out regularly with a friend, your spouse, or a family member certainly isn't a necessity, it can be a fantastic way to get in shape. If you've agreed to work out together, you'll be less likely to miss an exercise session or cut it short. But as my Hidden Hills workout club knows, there's another added benefit to exercising with a partner or a group. It makes fitness fun! And we could all use a little more fun in our lives.

Look at it another way—we're all so incredibly busy we barely have time to see our friends. If you make exercise "dates" or attend group classes, you can kill two birds with one stone: catching up with a pal *and* burning calories. It's also a great opportunity to trade some vices for some healthy activity. Instead of meeting for cocktails, how about a sunset stroll? For those of you who get bored with exercise, chatting during a power walk or hike will make the time fly by. You could even team up to do the program in this book together. You can help each other out with new moves and trade pep talks if the going gets tough. If you're having trouble coordinating schedules with your friends, another option is to sign up for a group class. Surrounded by fellow classmates, you'll be less likely to quit and more likely to give it your all.

I understand that finding the time to exercise can be a real challenge. All of us have obligations, commitments, deadlines, and on and on and on. That's why I love our Hidden Hills workouts. Because I'm the teacher, I can't roll over and hit the snooze button. On any given day, there are a handful of women who are counting on me to show up and lead the class. What's funny is that they think *I'm* the one providing the motivation. Little do they know that they're helping me stay in shape, too. Some mornings, it's my desire to inspire them that gets me out of bed and moving.

## Snack Attack

During my time at Jane Fonda's Laurel Springs Spa, Melanie Griffith, one of our regular guests, whipped up a fabulous broth that I've been making ever since. I love having it as a midafternoon snack, especially on a cold afternoon. Here's the simple recipe.  **Makes 6 1-cup servings**

6 cups water
2 chicken bouillon cubes
5 or 10 garlic cloves, peeled

1 bay leaf
Cayenne pepper to taste
1½ teaspoons olive oil

Fill up a medium-sized saucepan about ¾ full with water. Add the bouillon cubes, garlic cloves, and bay leaf. Shake in cayenne pepper until it covers the top of the water. Top with olive oil. Simmer until the garlic is soft, stirring occasionally. Ladle it into a cup and enjoy!

In addition to these weekly classes, I make time to do a 30-minute weight-lifting routine once or twice a week. Sometimes, when I'm working one-on-one with a client, we'll also go jogging or hiking. Otherwise my exercise typically comes in the form of "a little here and a little there." For example, when my kids are doing their homework, I might lie down on the floor and do abdominal exercises. I've been known to sneak in lunges and squats while waiting for a pot of water to boil. I frequently scrub the bathtub, run the vacuum, wash my car, or do another form of housework. (It can be a serious calorie-burning workout!) I also have a habit of moving furniture around in my house, which helps build strength.

Since we first started sweating and pumping iron together in our local community center, my neighbors have seen great results with my Hidden Hills workouts. That's why I want to share them with you. I can't transport you to sunny California to take my class in person, but I *can* give you the exercises to increase your energy, improve your balance, and develop a firmer, leaner body. Some of the regulars in my classes have dropped dress sizes, and so can you.

This is a high-energy workout, so I suggest turning on some upbeat music that makes you feel like moving. Good music can be better (and certainly healthier!) for invigorating your body than a shot of espresso. Turn on a great tune and you'll notice your toes tapping, your fingers

## D.J. Kathy's Recommendations

*The Dance Collection* (Casablanca Records), featuring Donna Summers' "I Feel Love" and "Last Dance"; Xscape's *Off the Hook,* with hit singles such as "Feels So Good" and "Do You Want To" (Sony Music); *1990s Dance Party* (Sony Music), with songs like "I Like It Like That" by the Blackout Allstars and "Gettin' Jiggy Wit It" by my neighbor Will Smith; and *Dance X-treme* (K-Tel International), featuring Maw and Co.'s "Gonna Get Back to You" and Clubland's "Set Me Free." Browse the mixed-collection section of your local music store and you'll find some great, get-your-groove-on discs.

snapping, and, even if you're sitting, your body swaying to the beat. You'll feel like dancing—and if you're ready to start dancing, you're ready to start working out. Put on your favorite CD or tune into your favorite radio station. Better yet, make your own mixed CD that includes lots of fun, energizing songs.

I often begin my classes with the song "September" by Earth, Wind and Fire. No one can possibly feel sluggish when it's playing. Actress Alfre Woodard, whom I train whenever she's in Los Angeles, loves anything with a strong drum beat, especially *Drums of Passion* by Babatunde Olatunji. "When I'm by myself in a motel room, I put on a compact disc with a rhythmic beat and jump around, shake my butt, and play," Alfre said to me the other day. "It's not about how many repetitions you do, you just have to move!"

# The Hidden Hills Workout

**THE PLAN**

Do this workout once a week on Wednesdays. **For cardio and strength:** To incinerate calories and sculpt your muscles, you'll be doing a combination of athletic-style drills, traditional weight moves, yoga exercises, and jump rope. Try to move quickly from one exercise to the next, so your heart doesn't have a chance to slow down.

## What You'll Need

- Playing cards
- Jump rope
- Watch with a timer
- Sturdy chair
- Light dumbbells (3 to 5 pounds)
- Pillow (optional)
- Stability ball
- Towel or exercise mat (optional)

## Warm-up

Before each workout, do my favorite Fitness Minute Warm-up, which some of you may remember seeing on the *Today* show. This energizing routine will get your blood circulating, your heart pumping, and your muscles ready to move.

**Knee to Elbow Touch.** Standing with your feet together, exhale as you lift your left knee up toward your chest, simultaneously bringing your right elbow over to touch your left knee. Return to starting position, then repeat with opposite knee and elbow. Do this 10 times.

**Jumping Jacks.** Standing with your feet together and your arms by your sides, exhale as you jump and separate your legs slightly wider than shoulder-width apart, simultaneously swinging your arms out to the side and up over your head. Jump back to starting position. Do this 10 times.

**Straight Leg Kicks.** Standing with your feet together, exhale as you kick your right leg straight in front of you, simultaneously reaching your left hand toward your right foot. Keep your back straight and don't lean forward. Return to starting position, then repeat with opposite arm and leg. Do this 10 times.

**Scissor Shuffle.** Standing with your left foot forward, exhale as you jump up and scissor your legs, so your feet are a few feet apart, right foot in front, left foot in back. Now, quickly jump and switch feet, so your left foot is in front, right foot in back. Pump your arms in opposition. Do this 10 times.

**Toe-Touch Clap Reach.** Standing with your feet together, exhale as you reach down with both hands and try to touch the floor (depending on how flexible you are, you may only be able to touch your shoes or your shins), keeping your knees slightly bent. Inhale as you come up and clap your hands in front of your chest, then exhale as you reach both arms over your head. Immediately lower your arms and clap your hands in front of your chest again. Do this 10 times at a quick pace.

**Punch the Sky.**  Stand with your feet wider than hip-width apart and your hands in fists, and punch your right hand toward the ceiling. Lower and repeat, punching your left hand to the ceiling. Do this 10 times.

Repeat all six moves. Now you should be ready to start your workout.

## The Workout

**1. Card Shuffle.** *You'll need some floor space for this drill. You'll be doing 3 or 4 shuffles to each side, then back again. Start with 5 cards, and gradually build up to 10.* Place your cards on the floor at the left end of the room. Stand with the cards directly in front of you, feet hip-width apart, chest lifted, belly button pulled in. Bend your knees to lower down into a squat and pick up one card. Stand back up, then shuffle to the right, stepping with your right foot first, then your left, until you've completed 3 to 4 shuffles. Squat down and place the card on the floor. Shuffle back to the pile of cards, and repeat. Continue this until all your cards are at the right end of the room. *Targets inner thighs; boosts your heart rate.*

**2. Squat-Thrust Jump Back.** Stand with your feet shoulder-width apart, chest lifted, and belly button pulled in. Exhale as you bend your knees to lower into a squat. Now, lower your chest down toward your knees and place your hands firmly on the floor in front of your feet. Jump both feet back into a push-up or plank position, so your hands are in line with your shoulders and your body weight is on your hands and the balls of your feet. Exhale as you bend your elbows and lower your torso to the floor to do a push-up. Inhale, then exhale as you press back up to a push-up position, then jump your feet back to your hands and straighten up. Do this 10 times. *Targets buttocks, hamstrings, quadriceps, shoulders, chest, triceps; boosts your heart rate.*

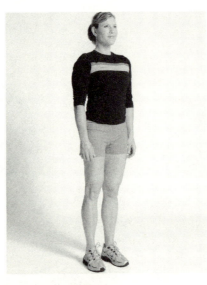

**3. Air Chair.** *This exercise is from my memory bank of drills done on athletic teams throughout high school and college. The air chair is just what it sounds like—sitting in a chair made of air. Well, almost.* Lean back against a sturdy wall. Step forward with both feet, so only your back is resting against the wall. Exhale as you slowly slide down the wall until you're in a squat position, with your hips level with your knees and your knees directly over your ankles. Breathe deeply and squeeze your buttocks together as you hold this position for 60 seconds, or as long as you can. To pass the time, you can sing a song, make a phone call, open your mail, or file your nails. *Targets buttocks, hamstrings, quadriceps.*

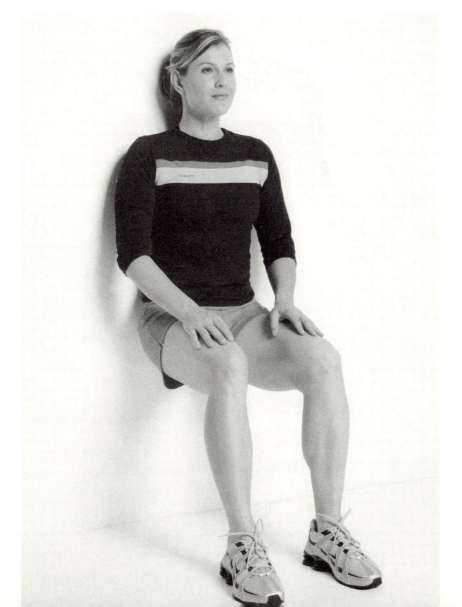

**4. Jump Rope.** *Use your watch to time yourself, or jump where you can see a clock with a second hand. Refer to Jump Rope Basics on page 72 for technique tips.* Start by doing three 1-minute intervals with 30-second rests in between. Gradually build up to three 1.5-minute sessions, then three 2-minute sessions. *Boosts your heart rate; targets quadriceps, biceps, calves.*

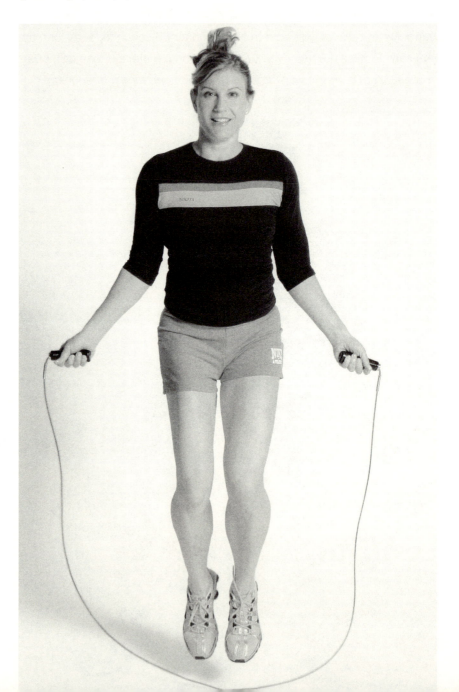

**5. a) Triceps Dip.** Sit on a sturdy chair with your hands on the front edge of the seat, fingers facing forward. (If the chair isn't sturdy enough, use a bench or coffee table instead.) Supporting yourself on your hands, walk your feet forward so your butt is in front of the chair seat, knees bent at 90-degree angles. Exhale as you slowly lower yourself down toward the floor, until your elbows are bent at 90-degree angles. Inhale, then exhale as you use your arms to push back up to starting position. Do this 10 times. *Targets triceps.*

**b) Reverse Fly.** Holding a light dumbbell in each hand, sit on the chair, then lean your upper torso forward so your chest rests upon your knees, and your arms hang down to the sides with the weights on the floor next to your feet. (For extra comfort and support, fold a pillow in half and place it on your lap.) Squeeze your shoulder blades together and pull your belly button in. You should form a straight line from your head to your tailbone. Now, keeping your back straight and elbows slightly bent, exhale as you raise your arms up and out to the side, slightly higher than shoulder level. Pause briefly, then inhale as you lower to starting position. Do this 10 times. *Targets upper back.*

After you've completed both exercises, rest for 30 to 60 seconds, then repeat the superset.

**6. Plank Reach and Hold.** Start in a straight-legged push-up or plank position, with your hands in line with your shoulders, hips lifted, legs extended behind you, body weight resting on your toes. Keeping your belly button pulled in, exhale as you reach forward with your right arm, simultaneously lifting your left leg off the floor. Breathe deeply as you hold for 10 seconds. Lower to starting position, then repeat with opposite arm and leg. Continue repeating until you have done 4 on each side. *Targets core muscles (abs and lower back).*

**7. Standing Broad Jump.** Place a piece of masking tape or a measuring tape on the floor. Stand facing the tape, with your feet hip-width apart, knees slightly bent, chest lifted, belly button pulled in. Extend both arms behind you with elbows slightly bent, then exhale as you jump as far as you can past the tape, landing on both feet with knees slightly bent. Mark your landing spot, then go back and do it again. Try to increase your distance every time. Start with 3 standing broad jumps, and gradually build up to 8. *Targets quadriceps, hamstrings, buttocks, calves.*

**8. a) Reverse Flat-Back Hold.** Sit on the floor with your calves supported on top of a stability ball, legs straight, hands on the floor behind you for support, fingers pointing back. Keeping your belly button pulled in and squeezing your buttocks, exhale as you press your hips up toward the ceiling. Your shoulders should be directly above your wrists. Pause briefly, then lower down to starting position. Do this 10 times. *Targets core muscles, shoulders, buttocks.*

**b) Ball Twist.** Sit on the floor with your legs extended in front of you, knees slightly bent, weight resting on your heels. Hold the stability ball in front of your chest. Keeping your buttocks firmly planted on the floor, lean back onto your tailbone and exhale as you rotate your upper torso to the left, moving the ball past your left hip and touching it to the floor. Pause, then rotate to your right side and touch the ball to the floor. Return to starting position. Do this 10 times, alternating sides. *Targets abdominals (inner and outer obliques).*

**9. Flutter Kick.** Lie on your belly with your arms folded in front of you, head resting on forearms, legs slightly apart, toes pointed. Keeping belly button pulled in and pressing down on your forearms, lift your legs off the floor and flutter kick them as if you were swimming, legs slightly apart. Breathe deeply as you do a total of 10 kicks with each leg. Rest for 30 seconds, then repeat twice. *Targets lower back, buttocks, hamstrings.*

**10. Downward Dog Push-up.** *This is a fun way to do push-ups, incorporating a popular yoga move that can really help improve the flexibility in your hamstrings.* Stand with your feet hip-width apart, chest lifted, belly button pulled in. Place your hands on the floor in front of your feet, as close to your body as possible. Keeping your heels on the floor, walk your hands forward until you feel a stretch in your hamstrings. Breathe deeply as you hold for a few counts. Continue walking your hands out as far as you can, lifting your heels, until you're in a straight-leg push-up or plank position. Do a push-up, then walk your hands back up to return to starting position. Do this 5 times, and gradually build up to 10. *Targets shoulders, chest, triceps, hamstrings, core muscles.*

## Cool-Down Stretches

Half Dog.  Stand about three or four feet away from a wall with your feet hip-width apart, chest lifted, belly button pulled in. Lean forward and place your hands on the wall at shoulder height and shoulder-width apart. Exhale as you slide your hands down the wall and flex at your hips, until your body forms an L, with your back flat like a tabletop and your arms straight. You should form a straight line from your buttocks to your shoulders to your hands. Keep your belly button pulled in and your neck in line with your spine. Breathe deeply as you hold for 30 seconds. Return to standing position, then repeat. *Stretches hamstrings, back, shoulders.*

# Panko-Breaded Chicken Breasts

For this healthy take on pan-fried chicken, Hollis Wilder uses Japanese bread crumbs, called *panko,* mixed with Parmesan cheese and sage, to create a rough, crunchy texture. You'll love the flavor! Panko is available in large supermarkets, specialty shops, and Asian groceries. If you'd like even more zing, serve the chicken with barbecue or honey mustard sauce.     **Makes 4 servings**

**Four boneless, skinless chicken breasts**
**1 large egg**
**1 cup Japanese bread crumbs (panko)**
**2 tablespoons Parmesan cheese, freshly grated**

**1 teaspoon fresh sage, minced**
**½ teaspoon salt**
**⅛ teaspoon freshly ground pepper**
**¼ cup extra-virgin olive oil**

1. Wash and pat dry the chicken breasts.

2. Lightly beat the egg in a shallow bowl.

3. Combine the bread crumbs with the Parmesan cheese, sage, salt, and pepper. Spread on a plate.

4. Dip each chicken breast into the egg, then press into the seasoned crumbs to coat.

5. In a large nonstick skillet, heat the olive oil until shimmering. Add the breasts and cook over medium heat, turning occasionally, until golden brown and cooked through, about 10 minutes.

6. Transfer the breasts to plates and serve.

**Legs on the Wall.** Lie on your back with your legs extended straight up against a wall and your buttocks as close to the wall crease as possible. (To get into this position, try sitting with your right side close to a wall, then lying back and pivoting your hips to the right as you extend your legs straight up.) Your arms are by your sides, with your palms facing up. Breathe deeply as you let your entire body relax and enjoy the moment. *Promotes total relaxation.*

**Pretzel Stretch.** Lie on your back about a foot and a half from the wall. Place both feet on the wall, knees bent at a 90-degree angle and in line with your hips. Cross your left ankle over your right knee, and exhale. You should feel the stretch deep in your left hip and buttock. Breathe deeply as you hold for 30 seconds, or as long as you can. Switch legs and repeat. *Stretches outer hip, upper and lower back, rear shoulder.*

If you have time, go back and do the Legs on the Wall stretch one more time. Then finish with the Extended Child's Pose.

**Extended Child's Pose.**  Start in an upright kneeling position. Sit back onto your heels, then lean forward and rest your forehead on the floor, arms extended straight in front of you. Allow your body to relax completely as you breathe deeply in through your nose and out through your mouth. Feel your diaphragm rising and falling as air goes in and out of your body. Let your muscles sink deeper into the floor with each breath. Stay in this pose for 10 full breaths, or as long as you like. *Soothes your lower back; rejuvenates and nurtures your body.*

# CHAPTER SEVEN

# The Pretty Woman Leg Workout
## . . . Starring Julia Roberts

*OK, I'll admit it: When Julia Roberts called* me looking for a personal trainer after landing her part in *America's Sweethearts*, I was elated! Even though I'd been lucky enough to work with many of Hollywood's top actresses, Julia seemed to be one of those stars who inhabited a different universe. Like so many others, I'd been a huge fan ever since she lit up the screen with her smile in *Pretty Woman*—and I was excited to finally get a chance to work with her.

Up close and in person, Julia is just as beautiful, if not more so, as she is on the big screen. She is a natural beauty, with gorgeous hair and flawless skin. She also is incredibly warm and friendly, and has a great sense of humor. She exudes happiness from the inside out. What she *isn't* is an image-obsessed Hollywood diva. She takes her workouts seriously, letting glamour take a backseat to comfort. She usually wears a T-shirt and inside-out sweatpants with her trademark locks pulled up and out of her face.

Since Julia was filming on location in Lake Meade, Nevada, just outside Las Vegas, I flew to the set about three times a week to train her. She was only going to be there a week or two, so I decided it would be easiest to commute back and forth. At the time, Julia hadn't been working out regularly. Her shooting schedule was hectic, and I could tell she was a little frazzled. She complained of feeling sluggish and wanted me to help boost her energy. This is always my favorite fitness goal, because it means my clients, like Julia, will get instant results.

" Exercising with Kathy has changed my life. Not in any huge 'tri-athlete' way, but in this great subtle and consistent way. I must admit, I don't love exercise, but I do love how I feel afterward and for the rest of the day. Accomplishment, clarity, energy, strength, joy. These are all things I give myself through working out, and I can feel it in everything I do. I have certainly noticed that when I don't work out I am tired and less focused and actually feel that I have cheated myself a bit. Seems like in the world today, everyone is so busy and in such a hurry and there is so much to do and only so many hours in a day; but are we really too busy to spend a little time every day taking care of ourselves? "

—**Julia Roberts**

## Workout Sneak Preview

Julia Roberts may have been born with beautiful, long legs, but she knows that good genes aren't going to keep them firm and toned. In this 25-minute routine, you'll be doing some of Julia's favorite moves for a sculpted lower body. It features yoga- and Pilates-inspired exercises as well as classic strength moves to strengthen and lengthen your muscles. Do this workout consistently, and you may soon be showing off your legs in shorts—or even a sexy miniskirt and high heels, à la Erin Brockovich.

## Honey Salad Dressing

Finding a healthy, low-fat salad dressing that actually tastes good can be a challenge. Thanks to Hollis Wilder, you can stop searching! With this combination of sweet honey, zesty spices, and mustard, you now have a terrific, tasty topping for your favorite salads.

**Makes 2½ cups**
**Serving size: 2 tablespoons**

⅔ cup sugar
1 teaspoon dry mustard
1 teaspoon paprika
1 teaspoon celery seed
¼ teaspoon salt

1 teaspoon white or yellow onion, grated
⅓ cup cider vinegar
⅓ cup honey
1 cup canola oil or other high-quality
    vegetable oil

In a small bowl, food processor, or blender, combine the sugar, mustard, paprika, celery seed, salt, onion, vinegar, and honey. Whisk or blend well. If using a bowl, slowly beat in the oil until the mixture emulsifies. If using a blender or food processor, engage the motor and slowly drizzle in the oil, blending until the mixture emulsifies. Use immediately, or cover and refrigerate up to 1 week. Return to room temperature and stir to blend before using.

As you can imagine, we had better odds of winning a slot-machine jackpot than finding a well-equipped gym in the middle of the Nevada desert. So, we got back to basics. On the first day I told Julia that we would need an exercise step, a jump rope, stretch bands, and a deck of cards for our training sessions. ("A deck of cards? Like playing cards?" she questioned me, clearly thinking I was looking for a blackjack game instead of a workout.)

Every time we worked out together, Julia and I tried to do something different. I incorporated as much variety as possible in order to keep it fun and interesting. For cardio, we would go hiking, do step aerobics, or use the jump rope. Each strength workout was designed to hit all of her major muscle groups. Some days, Julia wanted to work on a particular area of her body, such as her legs, so I would incorporate a few extra lower-body moves. We always took a few minutes to stretch at the end of each workout, whether we'd been hiking or doing sculpting exercises in her hotel room.

Unlike some of my other clients, Julia seemed to have a strong constitution from the beginning. I knew she was someone I could push, sometimes a little and sometimes a lot. She especially liked doing leg moves like lunges, a fantastic lower-body exercise that targets your thighs, buttocks, hips, and calves. Some of my trainees, as I like to call them, can do only one or two lunges on their first day, but Julia was able to do twenty of them. Sure, she grumbled a bit during the second set of ten (most people do!). But when her legs felt just a little sore the following day, she was happy. Just like the rest of us, she loves being able to feel when her muscles have been working hard.

It's easy to imagine that celebrities like Julia do everything perfectly right off the bat. Not true. When we started working together, she felt uncoordinated at times. Some of the exercises and stretches I suggested were a little awkward for her at first, and she'd laugh at herself when her body just wouldn't seem to go in a certain direction. Whether you're an Oscar-winning actress, a stay-at-home mom, or a serious athlete, it can take time to get the hang of new exercises. But Julia caught on quickly, and you will, too. So be patient. Remember what they say—practice makes perfect.

## You've Got Mail!

People always ask me if there is anything they would be surprised to know about Julia. The answer's no—she really is just so normal and down to earth. She even checks and answers her own e-mails:

TO: Kathy Kaehler

FROM: Julia Roberts

RE: Exercise

You will be happy to know I have been going to yoga for the last few weeks with regularity . . . I have been doing your "Your Best Body Target & Tone" tape for the last couple of days! It's a great way to spend 40 minutes and since it's you, it cracks me up and I feel like we are working out together.

Julia

When Julia told me she needed energy, I immediately knew that I needed to get her outside for some fresh air. So about once or twice a week, we would go hiking in the hills behind her hotel. Julia's friends (her hairdresser, makeup artist, and costume designer) usually joined us. Lake Meade was so beautiful. From the hiking trails we could see the sparkling sapphire water and the colorful rock formations surrounding it. On most days the overhead sky was bright blue and cloudless. And since it was winter, we weren't sweltering in the heat.

Our hikes typically lasted about an hour. Every time the hotel faded into the distance, Julia and her pals were convinced that we were going to get hopelessly lost. Without fail, one of them would say, "Kathy, they're going to have to send out a helicopter to come and find us!" Just for the record: Despite their lack of faith, we never lost our way, and no one was ever late for work.

Our daily hikes were fun and social, but they also provided an incredible workout. Hiking is a great way to improve your cardiovascular fitness while strengthening and sculpting your lower-body muscles. When you hike uphill, gravity creates resistance, so your heart and muscles have to work harder to propel you forward. Our outdoor adventures also provided a much-needed break from the hectic and often stressful atmosphere of

## Social Climbers

As we hiked all around Lake Meade, we had a blast talking, laughing, and joking with each other. All this chitchat was fun, but it also helped me determine if Julia and her friends were exercising within their target heart rates. To find out whether you're within your ideal range, take the "talk test" during your next cardio workout. You should be able to easily string at least three or four words together at all times. If you can't, you're working too hard. If you're able to sing a few verses from your favorite song without taking a breath, then you're not working out hard enough. Here's a suggestion: Try belting out "I Say a Little Prayer," one of the songs in Julia's hit movie *My Best Friend's Wedding*. If you don't miss a note, step up the intensity in your workout. Can't make it past the first chord? Ease up.

the movie set. Whether you're in a desert, in a forest, or on a beach, there's something calming and rejuvenating about just being outside.

In Lake Meade, Julia and I really hit it off. So a few months later, after the filming of *America's Sweethearts* had wrapped, she called and asked me to help her get ready for the Academy Awards. This wasn't just any Oscar ceremony—it was 2001, the year that Julia was nominated for Best Actress for her portrayal of tough-talking legal eagle Erin Brockovich. It was my job to help Julia look and feel her best when accepting the big award. (Maybe she didn't know she was going to win, but I had a feeling all along that she'd be holding an Oscar by the end of the night.)

Since she was planning to wear a sleeveless dress to the ceremony, Julia wanted to focus on her arms. So I added a few extra upper-body exercises to her program. We met as often as Julia's schedule allowed, and even worked out on the day of the big event. When our Oscar-day training session began, she was feeling great. But toward the end, she said that she was starting to feel butterflies in her stomach (and we both knew it wasn't from the ab routine we'd just done!). Later that evening, I was excited to see her onstage wearing her vintage Valentino (which ended up landing her on many best-dressed lists), smiling and holding the golden statuette. She looked fabulous—all her hard work really showed. And I'm sure that all of those biceps curls helped her raise her Oscar in victory.

When the Academy Awards were over, Julia immediately began filming her next movie, *Ocean's 11*. The film was set at the posh Bellagio Hotel in Las Vegas, and she wanted me to work with her for six weeks. Since I had three young children, I couldn't be away from home for long periods of time. My youngest son, Walker, was barely a year old! And commuting back and forth between Los Angeles and Las Vegas for six consecutive weeks would be too difficult. So I brought my kids and our nanny, Blanca, to the Bellagio Hotel for an extended visit. Talk about a great gig!

During the shoot, Julia stayed in a private villa reserved for "special guests." (Her esteemed costars—George Clooney, Brad Pitt, Matt Damon, and Andy Garcia, to name a few—were in neighboring villas.) Whenever it was time for her to work out, I would take an elevator to a special floor, where I was met by a butler who escorted me to Julia's villa. The villa's interior included a gigantic living room with extravagant floral arrangements and a full bar stocked with champagne flutes and crystal decanters. It also had a formal dining room, a full kitchen, several bedrooms, and a small fitness room with a treadmill and bicycle. The windows were adorned with heavy drapes, and multiple sets of double French doors opened up to a private pool.

On my first visit, I arrived to find Julia hanging out in her living room with George, Matt, and Andy. Naturally, I was a bit intimidated. But when I walked up, Julia introduced me to the group not as her trainer but as her friend, a gesture that indicates just how warm and kind she really is. As I stood there waiting for her, I was struck by how well the cast members all got along. There was a lot of laughter and playful banter, a dynamic that I think really came through in the film. During our training sessions, Julia regaled me with stories of her coworkers' practical jokes, which included ringing each other's doorbells and running away (not exactly the kind of cardio I typically prescribe, but every little bit helps).

One night, when Julia had other plans, she generously suggested that I bring my kids over to her villa to watch movies. No, she hadn't made a quick run to Blockbuster to rent videos. She had copies of all of the current

## Coffee Break: How to Kick the Habit for Good

I used to be a serious coffee junkie. Every morning I would go to the 7-Eleven, take a large cup, and fill it about three-quarters of the way full with flavored coffee. Then I'd fill the rest of the cup with Coffee-mate nondairy creamer (and not the fat-free kind!). I liked this morning ritual because it made waking up seem easier and gave me a jolt of energy. But it also gave me a jittery, anxious feeling that I didn't like, and I would often crash a few hours later. Deep down, I knew my coffee habit wasn't healthy. I wasn't sleeping enough, my schedule was running me ragged, and I was using caffeine to stimulate my body. As I mentioned earlier, caffeine is a drug, and it's addictive. It not only gives you a false sense of energy, it increases dehydration and can leech calcium from your bones. Finally, after a health scare about fifteen years ago, I decided to give it up. I couldn't go cold turkey without getting a headache, so I

gradually weaned myself off it. To slowly reduce my caffeine intake, I started mixing a small amount of decaf into my cup. At the beginning of each week, I would increase the ratio of decaffeinated to regular coffee. After about six weeks, I was drinking only decaf. I felt a bit sluggish for a week or two, but my natural energy system soon kicked in. These days, I rely on the best natural stimulant—exercise—to keep myself energized. I also drink a lot of water and eat plenty of complex carbohydrates, including whole grains, fresh fruits, and vegetables, to invigorate me. Because my body is no longer jacked up on caffeine, I sleep better and feel more rested. I rarely crave coffee anymore. But when I do have an urge for a warm drink and the smell of roasted beans, I hit my local coffee bar for a latte with one shot of decaf espresso, steamed fat-free milk, and "extra foam" in a large cup.

Academy Award–nominated films, many of which were still playing in theaters. The tapes had been sent to Academy members, like Julia, for consideration. So we lounged around in Julia's suite like movie stars, pretending we were members of the Academy and watching *Monsters, Inc.* What fun!

During our time at the Bellagio, I often ran to Wild Oats Market to stock Julia's refrigerator with healthy snacks: protein bars, carrot and other fresh, organic juices, dried fruit, precut fresh fruits and veggies, and Pirate

Booty. At the time, Julia loved coffee, so after working out she would often grab a cup of java. I talked to Julia about cutting back on her caffeine intake, as I often do with clients. For example, rather than ordering a drink with three shots of espresso, I suggested asking for one shot of regular espresso and two shots of decaf in a large cup. By filling the rest of the cup with steamed fat-free milk and foam, she'd also get a bone-fortifying boost of calcium.

By the time *Ocean's 11* was winding down, Julia and I had developed a great workout relationship. So after we got back from Las Vegas, she asked me to accompany her to Illinois, where she was filming a documentary called *Old Friends*. It was the spring of 2002, just two months before she married cameraman Danny Moder in a secret Fourth of July ceremony on her New Mexico ranch. The documentary was about three women, each more than a hundred years old, who had been friends their entire lives. Julia had signed on to be the host of the documentary because she felt so passionate about the subject.

## Stellar Snacks on the Go

Whenever I leave home, I try to carry a few healthy snacks with me. That way, if I'm hungry or getting low in energy, I won't crash or hit the fast-food drive-through. But at times when I don't have nutritious nibbles stashed in my shoulder bag, I can usually find something quick and healthy at a convenience store, as I did when I was on the road with Julia. Here are a few examples:

Hard-boiled eggs

Unsalted nuts

Sunflower or sesame seeds

Mozzarella sticks

Beef jerky

Wheat crackers

Fresh fruit such as an apple or banana

Raisins, apricots, apples, or other dried fruit

Low-sodium V8

Fresh-squeezed juice

Unsalted oat bran pretzels

Yogurt

Pirate Booty

After traveling by plane and car to a small town outside of Chicago, Julia spent an entire day interviewing subjects at a local park. She never took a break! By three o'clock in the afternoon, my blood sugar was plummeting, and I figured hers was, too. We hadn't eaten since breakfast, so I decided that we needed to get some food. As I've already explained, it's important to eat consistently throughout the day to keep your metabolism charged and prevent blood-sugar dips that can cause you to binge on unhealthy foods. However, we were in a tiny town with nothing but a gas station. There were no supermarkets or restaurants in sight.

Fortunately, in the station's mini-mart, I did manage to find a few nutritious options. I bought a few containers of hard-boiled eggs, wheat crackers, beef jerky, sesame seeds, and orange juice. We spread out the fare on the roof of our rental car and had an impromptu picnic. The moral? There are *always* smart food choices to make, whether you're in rural Illinois, at a highway rest stop, or in the airport waiting for a flight.

After we returned to Los Angeles, Julia and I began meeting four times a week at 8 A.M. to continue her training. Our early-morning sessions usually lasted about forty-five minutes. I continued trying to keep each session fresh and fun, and it really seemed to be paying off. By now, Julia was in great shape and excited to work out regularly. What more could I ask for?

As you've already learned, you don't need a lot of fancy equipment to get a great workout, and my experience with Julia was a prime example of that. Between her room at the Bellagio Hotel, a gym in Chicago, and her home in Los Angeles, I'd had to adapt Julia's workouts to many different settings and schedules. The Pretty Woman Leg Workout that follows is equally simple and adaptable. All you'll need is a 12-inch platform, a stability ball, and a medium-sized ball.

This routine is based on the multitude of workouts that Julia and I have done over the five years we've known each other. It's designed to strengthen and lengthen all of your lower-body muscles, but especially your legs. You'll sculpt the front of your thighs (your quadriceps); tone your inner and outer thighs; and define the back of your thighs—a.k.a. your hamstrings, or what my *Today* show colleague Ann Curry calls the "hammies."

With these exercises, you'll also target the lower part of your buttocks, or your gluteus maximus, which some women call the "ledge." This is a region that I hear my clients complain about all the time. The gluteus maximus is a large muscle; if you don't work on strengthening it, it's going to droop. By doing these moves once a week, you can lift and firm this problem area so you feel sexy and svelte in your favorite jeans.

# The Pretty Woman Leg Workout

D o this workout once a week on Thursdays. With these moves, you'll really feel your muscles working! Some of the exercises require holding your body in a pose to boost your muscular endurance. You'll increase your range of motion and body awareness while using your core muscles to maintain balance and alignment. You'll learn how to control and isolate your target muscles for Oscar-worthy results: shapely legs and firm buttocks.

## What You'll Need:

- 12-inch platform (a sturdy low chair, step stool or bench, or a step aerobics bench with three risers)
- Stability ball
- Medium-sized ball
- 3-pound dumbbells (optional)
- Towel or exercise mat (optional)

## Warm-up

**Step Together Reach.** Stand with your feet together, your chest lifted, and your belly button pulled in. Take a big step to the right with your right foot. As you step on your right foot, bring the left foot to join the right. Reach up as high as you can with your left arm, feeling the stretch all the way down the left side of your body. Repeat, stepping to your left side and reaching up with your right arm. Do this 10 times.

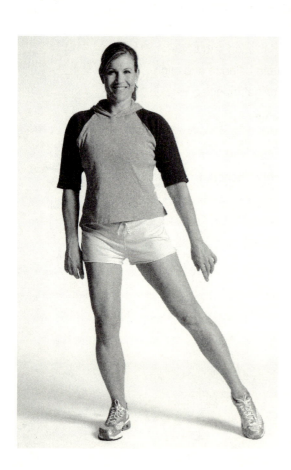

**March in Place.**  Stand with your feet hip-width apart, your chest lifted, and your belly button pulled in. Lift up one knee at a time as high as you can, simultaneously pumping your elbows. Do this until you have done 20 lifts with each knee.

**Side-Step Cross-Back.** Step to the right with your right foot, then step your left foot back behind your right leg, simultaneously extending your left arm straight out in front of you. Repeat, stepping to the left, crossing back with your right foot, and extending your right arm. Do this 10 times.

Repeat March in Place.

When you're finished, stand tall, then inhale as you sweep your arms out to the side and up above your head. Exhale as you sweep arms back down to starting position. Do this 3 times.

Now you should be ready to start your workout.

## The Workout

1. a) **Warrior Pose.** Stand with your feet hip-width apart, chest lifted, belly button pulled in. Exhale as you take a large step forward with your left foot and lower your left knee into a partial lunge, keeping your right leg straight and turning your right foot out 45 degrees; your left knee should be in line with your left toes. Now, turn your hips to face the right side of the room. Exhale as you extend your arms out to the sides at shoulder height, keeping your shoulders down, and look toward your left hand. Breathe deeply as you hold for 10 seconds. Switch sides and repeat. *Targets buttocks, quadriceps, hamstrings, abdominals, shoulders, calves.*

**b) Twisting Lunge.** Standing tall, exhale as you take a large step forward with your right foot, bending your right knee so it is directly above your right ankle; your left knee should be slightly bent, with the left heel lifted. Press your palms together in front of your chest, then exhale as you lean forward and twist to the right, placing the back of your left arm on the outside of your right knee. Breathe deeply as you hold for 10 seconds. Straighten your legs to return to starting position. Switch legs and repeat. Do this 3 times. *Targets buttocks, quadriceps, hamstrings, hips; stretches waistline and chest.*

**2. Ball Wall Squat.** *To make this move more challenging, hold a 3-pound dumbbell in each hand. As you get stronger, switch to heavier weights.* Stand with a stability ball between the wall and your lower back, feet hip-width apart, toes facing forward. Exhale as you bend your knees and lower your hips until they're slightly above your knees, tilting your hips back toward the wall as you lower. Pause, then exhale as you push up through your heels to return to starting position. Start by doing 10 squats, and gradually build up to 20. *Targets buttocks, hamstrings, quadriceps.*

**3. Step Up.** *Start by using a sturdy 12-inch platform for this move. You can use a low chair, step stool, or bench, or a step aerobics bench with three risers. To make it even more challenging, switch to a higher platform. To make it easier, use a lower platform.* Place your platform next to the wall; if you're using a chair, the seat should be facing away from the wall. Stand facing the platform with your chest lifted, belly button pulled in. Place your left foot on the center of the platform. Holding the wall for support, exhale as you rise up to tap the chair seat with your right foot. (Eventually you should be able to do this move without holding on to the wall.) Then, lower yourself down to starting position. Keep the movement slow and controlled. Do this 10 times, then switch legs and repeat. Focus on using your target muscles—your hamstrings, quadriceps, and buttocks—to do the work. *Targets hamstrings, quadriceps, buttocks; elevates heart rate.*

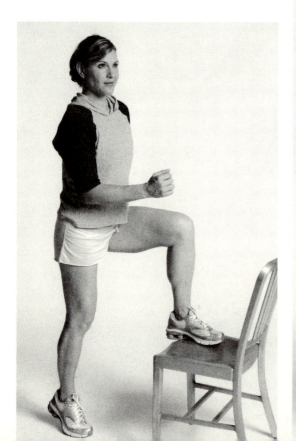

**4. T-Pose Butt Shaper.**  Holding 10 playing cards in your left hand, stand with your feet together, knees slightly bent, chest lifted, belly button pulled in. Keeping your left leg slightly bent and hands in front of your chest, exhale as you lift your right leg back and lower your torso forward, until your body forms a T. Maintaining the pose and keeping your belly button pulled in, deal one card onto the floor in front of you with your right hand. Slowly lower leg and return to standing position. Repeat until all cards have been dealt. Then switch legs and repeat, this time picking up the cards one at a time. *Targets buttocks, abdominals, back, arms; improves balance.*

**5. Big-Ball Twisting Lunge.** Stand with your feet hip-width apart, chest lifted, belly button pulled in. Hold the stability ball with arms extended in front of your chest, perpendicular to your body. Exhale as you take a large step forward with your right foot, bending both knees so your right knee is directly above your right ankle and your left knee approaches the floor, left heel lifted. Hold the lunge and twist your upper torso as far as you can to the left, keeping your arms straight. Pause, then return to starting position. Switch sides and repeat so you're lunging with your left leg and twisting your torso to the right. Do a total of 8 to 10 twisting lunges on each side. *Targets quadriceps, hamstrings, buttocks; stretches your torso.*

**6. Outer Thigh Lift.** Kneel on the floor with the stability ball next to your right hip. Keeping your right knee on the floor and placing both hands on the front of the ball for support, lean your right hip into the ball and extend your left leg out to the side, with your left foot resting on the floor. Now, exhale as you slowly lift your left leg until it is parallel to the floor, knee facing forward. Don't let your hips roll forward or back as you lift. Inhale as you lower your leg down to starting position. Do this 15 times. Switch sides and repeat. *Targets outer thighs.*

**7. Inner-Thigh Straddle Slimmer.** Lie on your back with a medium-sized ball under your tailbone, legs extended straight up in the air, with your toes turned out and your arms by your sides. Keeping your legs straight and your belly button pulled in, exhale as you flex your feet and open your legs out to the sides in a wide V. Inhale as you return legs to starting position, touching your heels together. Do this 10 times. Rest for 30 to 60 seconds, then repeat. *Targets inner thighs.*

**8. Hip Lift with Ball.** Lie on your back with your knees bent, feet hip-width apart and flat on the floor, arms by your sides. Place a small ball between your knees. Squeeze the ball with your knees to isolate your inner thigh muscles. Now, inhale as you lift your hips off the floor into a bridge pose so your shoulders, abs, and knees form one straight line. Don't drop the ball! Squeeze your buttocks, then exhale as you roll your spine back down to starting position. Start by doing 10, and build up to 15. *Targets buttocks, hamstrings, inner thighs.*

**9. Leg Circles.** Lie on your back with your left leg extended straight up toward the ceiling and your right knee bent, with your right foot flat on floor and your arms by your sides. Turn out your left leg so your kneecap faces to the left, then exhale as you lower your leg down as far as you can, without lifting your lower back off the floor. Now, keep your right hip pressed into the floor and breathe deeply as you circle your left leg counterclockwise, drawing a large circle in the air with your left foot. Do 8 leg circles. Repeat with your opposite leg. *Targets inner thighs, quadriceps, abdominals.*

**10. Twisted Torso.** Lie on your back with both knees bent and your feet raised off the floor. Your knees are slightly in front of your hips and your arms are extended out to the sides at shoulder level, palms facing down. (For more support, place your hands under your hips.) Keeping your head, shoulders, and upper back on the floor, slowly bring both knees across your body and down toward the floor, lowering them as far as you can toward the floor. Pause, then exhale as you lift your knees back up and to the center. Repeat on the opposite side. Start by doing 5 on each side, and build up to 8 on each side. *Targets hip flexors, back, abdominals (inner and outer obliques).*

## Cool-Down Stretches

**Hip and Back Roll.**  Lie on your back with your left knee bent and your right leg extended straight out on the floor. Your left arm is extended out to the side and your right hand is on the outside of your left knee. Exhale as you pull your knee across your body and down to the floor by your right hip. Feel the stretch in your left hip and lower back. Breathe deeply as you hold for 30 seconds. Switch sides and repeat. *Stretches hips and lower back.*

**Straight Leg Stretch.** Lie on your back with your right knee bent and your left leg extended straight out on the floor. Exhale as you raise your right leg, keeping your knee slightly bent, straight up over your right hip. Clasp your hands behind your right knee and, without lifting your back or buttocks off the floor, gently pull your right leg in toward your chest until you feel a stretch along the back of your right thigh. Breathe deeply as you hold for at least 30 seconds, or as long as you can. Switch legs and repeat. *Stretches hamstrings.*

**Body Ball.** Still lying on your back, hug your knees into your chest, wrapping your arms around your thighs behind your knees. Gently lift your head up and tuck your chin into your chest. Hold for a few seconds, then relax, keeping your knees tucked into your chest. Do this 4 times, breathing deeply in through your nose and out through your mouth. Let all your muscles relax. *Stretches buttocks, lower back, upper back, shoulders.*

# Chicken with Olive-Wine Sauce

Leave it to Carrie Wiatt to create a recipe that combines three heart-healthy ingredients—red wine, olives, and garlic—for a fabulously flavorful sauce. In addition to chicken, you can serve this sauce with any grilled, baked, or broiled fish or poultry for a quick, low-fat, and delicious meal—and the sauce is only 52 calories per serving!

**Makes 4 servings**

4 boneless chicken breasts (about 1 pound)
1¼ tablespoons black olives, pitted
2 teaspoons olive oil
1¼ tablespoons garlic, chopped
2 tablespoons fresh rosemary, chopped fine

1 cup dry red wine
1½ cups low-sodium chicken broth
2 tablespoons arrowroot powder
Cooking spray

1. Pour olive oil in a shallow dish with half of the garlic and 1 tablespoon of the rosemary.

2. Marinate the chicken in the flavored oil 2 hours or overnight.

3. Put olives in a food processor to make a paste. Set aside.

4. Spray cooking spray in a brassier pan over medium-high heat. Sauté the chicken until brown on both sides (approximately 4 minutes on each side). Transfer to a plate, cover, and keep warm. Set aside.

5. In the brassier pan, add the wine and chicken broth and cook, stirring constantly to loosen cooked-on brown bits. Add remaining rosemary, olive paste, and remaining garlic, and cook until liquid is reduced by half.

6. Dilute arrowroot powder in a bit of water and add to sauce. Stir until slightly thickened, about 1 minute.

**Child's Pose with Extended Leg.** Start in an upright kneeling position. Sit back onto your heels, place your arms in front of you, and lean forward and rest your forehead on the backs of your hands. Slowly extend your right leg back behind you and hold. Allow your body to relax completely as you breathe deeply in through your nose and out through your mouth. Feel your diaphragm rising and falling as air goes in and out of your body. Let your muscles sink deeper into the floor with each breath. Stay in this pose for 10 full breaths, or as long as you like. Repeat pose, extending left leg. *Soothes your lower back; rejuvenates and nurtures your body.*

# CHAPTER EIGHT

# The Charlie's Angels Boot Camp Workout

## . . . Starring Drew Barrymore

**W**hen I met Drew in the fall of 1998, she was getting ready to shoot the first *Charlie's Angels* movie. She knew that her role as Dylan Sanders was going to involve a lot of physically challenging stunts (not to mention skimpy outfits!). While she would be working with a martial arts expert and a stunt training team during production, she wanted to start preparing her body for the part. Her goals were to get stronger and fitter, look more toned, and shed some of those excess pounds.

Drew and I worked out together for about eight weeks before the filming began. About three or four times a week, I drove to her house in a beautiful area known as Coldwater Canyon, on the border of Beverly Hills. The hillside property was large and gorgeous, with lush landscaping, a tennis court, and a pool. Her two-story house had dark wood shingles and a rustic look. (Sadly, this handsome house was destroyed by a fire a few years later.) In addition to the main house, there was a guest house and a big garage with rooms above it.

In one of these spacious, above-garage rooms, Drew had a workout area with a stationary bike and a set of dumbbells. She also had a Pilates Reformer, a rectangular piece of equipment with springs and pulleys designed for exercising against resistance. Other than Pilates, Drew hadn't been able to find a workout that she really enjoyed. Consequently, she hadn't been sticking to a regular exercise program or getting the results that she wanted.

## Workout Sneak Preview

Before filming the movie version of *Charlie's Angels,* Drew Barrymore recruited me to help her get in shape for her role as butt-kicking Angel Dylan Sanders. This combination of calorie-incinerating cardio and boot camp–inspired exercises is based on the weekly workouts that we did together. It will leave you feeling lean, strong, energized, and ready to take on the bad guys!

Drew told me that part of the problem was the size of her chest, which made any type of high-impact exercise, such as running and step aerobics, uncomfortable. So I told her about a wonderful sports bra from a company called Enell (www.enell.com). The bra, which has a hook-and-eye closure, is incredibly supportive and really "straps you in." She thought it sounded great and ordered one. When the bra arrived and she put it on, Drew was incredibly happy and relieved. I remember her saying, "This bra is going to change my life!" And I don't think she was being dramatic. It's amazing what a difference proper workout attire can make.

Back then, Drew was a devout vegetarian. She ate lots of organic vegetables, fruits, grains, and soy products. When Thanksgiving rolled around, she told me that she was going to serve a "tofurkey" (a turkey made out of tofu) to her guests. (Now *that's* a dedicated veggie!). While Drew was con-

## Buckwheat Noodle Salad with Tamari Dressing

Hollis Wilder knows how busy we are. That's why she created this easy, super-satisfying salad. The noodles cook in only 6 minutes, which is just enough time to do 20 lunges! **Makes 4 servings**

10.5-ounce package soba noodles
(Japanese-style buckwheat noodles)
½ cup tamari
2 tablespoons fresh lemon juice
1 tablespoon golden brown sugar
1 tablespoon prepared white horseradish
1 tablespoon minced fresh ginger

¾ cup cucumber, peeled and cut into thin strips
¾ cup carrots, peeled and cut into thin strips
¾ cup red bell pepper, cut into thin strips
¾ cup green onions, cut into thin strips

1. Cook noodles in a large pot of boiling salted water until tender but still firm, stirring occasionally, about 6 minutes. Transfer noodles to bowl of ice water to cool quickly. Drain well.

2. Whisk tamari, lemon juice, brown sugar, horseradish, and ginger in small bowl until sugar dissolves. Combine noodles and tamari dressing in a separate bowl; toss to coat. Season with salt and pepper. (Note: You can make this salad up to 4 hours ahead. Cover and refrigerate. Toss before serving.)

3. Arrange cucumber, carrots, bell pepper, and onions on top of noodles and serve.

## The Secret to Living Longer

If your workouts aren't slimming you as quickly as you would like, take heart: They're adding years to your life. A study at the prestigious Cooper Institute for Aerobics Research in Dallas found that cardiorespiratory fitness may be a better predictor of mortality than your body size and weight. So rather than obsessing over the scale, stay focused on all the incredible things that you're doing for your health.

suming plenty of fruits and vegetables, I reminded her to be sure to get enough protein from sources like soy, nuts, seeds, beans, eggs, and dairy products. She had a bad habit of skipping meals. I explained that by eating more regularly, she could stay better fueled for her busy days and keep her metabolism super-charged.

Drew is also a serious animal lover. Aside from volunteering and donating money to animal charities, she has personally rescued many animals. At the time, she had about four adopted dogs and a few roosters under her care. Whenever I arrived at her front door, I was greeted by a bunch of wagging tails. As Drew and I made our way to her exercise room, her dogs would follow us, then stand outside the paned glass door watching intently as we worked out. Talk about adoring fans!

To help Drew blast calories and boost her fitness level, I put together a boot camp–style circuit workout for her. The goal was to elevate her heart rate while strengthening and toning her muscles. During these training sessions I kept her moving, incorporating as many different exercises as possible to engage more muscles and keep her from getting bored. Without stopping, she alternated between strength moves like squat jumps and power lunges, and cardio activities such as jump rope and jumping jacks. She also did athletic drills, such as side-to-side shuffles and line sprints. Because she has such youthful energy and spirit, I thought she'd enjoy a workout that allowed her to feel like a kid again. Since she was doing exercises that were new to her muscles, I knew her body would respond well—and it did.

During these intense, heart-pumping workouts, Drew was a real trooper. She never whined or complained. Her energy level was high, and she was always ready for whatever I had in store for her. Despite her Hollywood upbringing, Drew has a real girl-next-door quality. She was always fun and very friendly, with a genuine joie de vivre. We would chat about our lives, and she would ask lots of questions about my children, my husband, and my other activities. After getting to know her, I can understand why she's been cast as a sweet, down-to-earth girl in movies such as *Ever After* and *Never Been Kissed*.

When I finally saw *Charlie's Angels*, I thought her body looked fantastic. But I was even more impressed three years later when I saw her in the sequel, *Charlie's Angels: Full Throttle.* I was no longer training her, but I could tell she'd been keeping up on her workouts. It's obvious that she's found activities she loves and has made exercise a regular part of her lifestyle. Plus, as she put it in a recent *People* magazine article, "I finally found a great jogging bra, too—and that has a lot to do with [me getting in shape]."

Since Drew began exercising regularly, her body has changed dramatically. But even with her impressive weight loss, she still looks healthy and voluptuous. I love the fact that she flaunts her feminine curves rather than try to hide them. While she likes being fit, Drew isn't willing to starve herself to be stick thin, and she's accepting of the body she's been given. As I explained in Chapter 1, this kind of body confidence is something we should all strive for. And research shows that exercise is one of the most effective mechanisms for improving your self-image.

The Charlie's Angels Boot Camp Workout is the ideal way to end a stressful week. It's fast-paced, so you'll really feel your heart thumping and work up a good sweat. Got a problem at work? Misbehaving kids? Stuck in traffic? After doing this workout, you should feel stronger and better able to cope with daily aggravations. It will allow you to give whatever's bugging you a good kick in the pants and assert your own power and strength. Best of all, you'll head into your weekend with more energy, self-esteem, and color in your cheeks.

# The Charlie's Angels Boot Camp Workout

**THE PLAN**

Do this workout once a week on Fridays. **For cardio:** You'll be doing a 30-minute, fat-blasting cardio circuit that includes walking, jogging, and jumping rope. **For strength:** You'll do an intense 20-minute boot camp–style workout that incorporates proven strength moves, athletic drills, and kickboxing to burn calories, firm your muscles, and build coordination, agility, and power.

## What You'll Need

- Watch with a timer
- Jump rope
- Sturdy chair or coffee table
- Small wastebasket (or a laundry basket, box, stack of towels, or portable bench)
- Dumbbells (5 and 8 pounds)
- Stability ball
- Masking tape
- Low (1- or 2-inch) platform, such as a step aerobics bench or two hardcover books
- Towel or exercise mat (optional)

L ike the cardio portion of The Supermodel Lower-Body Conditioner, this interval program combines walking and jumping rope; however, this time you'll be adding jogging to the mix. Doing so will allow you to work at a higher intensity for a longer period of time, which means even more calories burned. Once again, you'll be alternating between higher-intensity and lower-intensity (or "recovery") spurts of exercise—an effective way to challenge your heart without overtaxing yourself.

Here's how it works: You'll do 2 or 3 minutes of brisk walking followed by 1 or 2 minutes of jogging and 1 minute of jump rope (this equals 1 interval). Continue repeating each 5-minute interval for 30 minutes, or until you've gone 2 miles. At the end of your workout, cool down by walking slowly for 3 to 5 minutes, or until your heart rate has slowed down.

Aim to walk at a brisk pace (about 15 minutes per mile, or 4 miles per hour), like you did in The Supermodel Lower-Body Conditioner. Jog at a moderate pace (at least 11 to 12 minutes per mile, or 5 miles per hour). If you can't walk or jog this fast, work on gradually increasing your speed. If you already walk at these prescribed speeds, continue working on picking up the pace. As you get more fit, you can also lengthen the jogging intervals, or decrease the walking intervals, so you're jogging more and walking less.

Before getting started, study the intervals outlined below, or make a copy and carry it with you. Tie your jump rope around your waist. Wear a watch with a timer (or bring a stopwatch) to time your intervals. Put on comfortable walking shoes or cross-trainers. Now you should be ready to go!

Here's how the intervals break down:

Minutes 1–3: Walk

Minute 4: Jog

Minute 5: Jump rope

Repeat

Minutes 11–12: Walk

Minutes 13–14: Jog

Minute 15: Jump rope

Repeat

Minutes 21–23: Walk

Minute 24: Jog

Minute 25: Jump rope

Repeat

Cool down: 3 to 5 minutes of slow walking

For maximum results and injury prevention, be sure your muscles are warm before starting each strength workout. Either do the warm-up outlined below or perform the strength exercises immediately after your cardio workout. Rest 15 to 60 seconds between exercises, depending on how you feel. End by doing the cool-down stretches on pages 198–200.

**STRENGTH**

## Warm-up

March in Place. Stand with your feet hip-width apart, arms by your sides, chest lifted, belly button pulled in. Lift one knee at a time as high as possible while swinging your arms, elbows bent at 90 degrees. Do this 20 times.

**Side Steps.** Stand with your feet together, chest lifted, and belly button pulled in. Take a giant step to the right with your right foot, then your left foot, simultaneously extending your arms out to both sides. Lower your arms, then repeat the move, stepping to the left. Do this 20 times.

Repeat both moves, then do 10 jumping jacks. Repeat the entire sequence once, and you should be ready to start your workout.

## The Workout

**1. Squat Jump/Lunge Combo.**  Stand with your feet shoulder-width apart, chest lifted, belly button pulled in. Bend your knees into a squat, then jump up in the air, simultaneously reaching your arms straight up toward the ceiling. Land in a squat position, then straighten your legs to return to standing position. Step forward with your right foot, then exhale as you bend both knees into a lunge, so your right thigh is parallel to the floor and your left knee points down, left heel lifted. Your right knee should be directly over your right ankle. Push back to starting position, then step forward with your left foot and bend both knees into a lunge. Straighten up and return to starting position. Repeat the entire sequence for a total of 8 times. *Targets buttocks, quadriceps, hamstrings, calves, core muscles (abs and back); boosts heart rate.*

**2. Box Jump-Over.** Place a sturdy chair up against a wall, seat facing toward you, and a small wastebasket upside down (you can also use a laundry basket or box, or even a step aerobics bench) on the floor about a foot or two from the front of the chair. Standing facing the chair and to the right of the wastebasket, and place your hands on the edge of the seat, then lean forward so your shoulders are directly over your wrists. Exhale and squeeze your legs together as you jump over the wastebasket, keeping your body weight on your hands. Repeat, jumping to the right, back over the basket. Take off and land with your feet together, using momentum to help propel you into your next jump. Do this 20 times (10 jumps to each side). *Targets shoulders, quadriceps, hamstrings, calves, buttocks.*

**3. Plyo Push-up with a Clap.** Lie facedown on the floor with your knees bent, your feet lifted above your knees, and your hands on the floor slightly wider than shoulder-width apart. Keep your head, neck, and back in a straight line, with your belly button pulled in. Push up, using momentum to propel you up off the floor, and clap your hands in the air. Land on your hands and lower yourself down for the next plyo push-up. If you can't clap in between, do a regular push-up. Start with 2 sets of 5 and work up to 2 sets of 10. *Targets triceps, chest, shoulders.*

**4. Jumping Jacks.** *Jumping jacks have been in my exercise repertoire for as long as I can remember. Because both your arms and legs are involved, they get your blood pumping through your entire body. A few sets of jumping jacks can raise your pulse as much as an aerobics class. Plus, they're incredibly simple and easy to do. That's why they're a staple in many boot camp workouts — and I've added them to yours.* Stand with your feet together, arms by your sides, chest lifted, belly button pulled in. Exhale as you jump and separate your legs slightly wider than shoulder-width apart, simultaneously swinging your arms out to the side and up over your head. Jump back to starting position. Do this 20 times. *Targets quadriceps, buttocks, shoulders; boosts your heart rate.*

**5. a) Pike on Ball.** *If this exercise is too challenging, modify it by bending your knees as you lift your hips.* Lie on top of a stability ball, with your hands on the floor in front of you and your belly button pulled in. Walk your hands forward until your knees are resting on the center of the ball, keeping your arms straight, your wrists in line with your shoulders. Your body should form a straight line from your head to your toes. Keeping your legs and torso straight and belly button pulled in, exhale as you lift your hips into a pike position or inverted V, so the ball rolls down along your shins. Slowly return to the starting position. Start by doing 5, and gradually work up to 15. *Targets core muscles (abs and back), some biceps, shoulders, chest; improves balance.*

**b) Freeze and Shoot.** *I love this move because it makes me feel like a Charlie's Angel! Pretend you're holding a gun, and aim it at an imaginary villain and fire away!* Lie faceup on the stability ball in a "table" position, with your shoulders and head supported on top of the ball and your knees bent, feet flat on the floor, buttocks lifted. Extend your arms straight up and interlace your fingers, pointing your index fingers upward and looking up at your hands. Keeping your arms locked, exhale as you lift your left shoulder up off the ball, shift your upper body to the right, and drop your hands to the right so you're aiming toward the right wall. Your left shoulder should be directly over your right shoulder. Return to starting position. Repeat the move, shifting to the left and aiming at the left wall. Do this 5 times on each side. *Targets core muscles, buttocks, quadriceps.*

**6. Dead Lift.** *This move is performed standing on a low platform, such as an exercise step or two hardcover books. This will allow you to lower the weights slightly below your feet, which makes the exercise more effective. Be sure to squeeze your buttocks as you return to standing position; this will help you engage your lower body and prevent lower back strain. Start by using your light weights; after 3 to 4 weeks, or as soon as you're ready, switch to your heavy weights.* Holding a dumbbell in each hand, stand on a sturdy low platform with your feet hip-width apart, weights in front of your thighs. Lift your chest and pull your belly button in. With your knees slightly bent and a slightly rounded back, bend forward at your hips and lower your torso toward the floor as far as you can. You should feel the stretch in your hamstrings. Pause, then exhale as you squeeze your buttocks together and lift your torso back to starting position, keeping your back straight. Focus on using your hamstrings and buttocks to get you back up. Start by doing this 8 times, and work up to 12 times. *Targets hamstrings.*

**7. Crab Walk.** *You'll need about 20 to 30 feet of floor space for this drill. A long hallway is an ideal place to do it.* Sit on the floor with your knees bent, feet flat on the floor, hands on the floor behind you, fingers pointing toward you. Lift your buttocks off the floor, using your hands and feet for support. Crab walk backward as fast as you can, keeping your butt lifted and your belly button pulled in, for 20 counts (1 count equals each time you move a hand). Turn around and return to starting position. *Targets shoulders, triceps, buttocks, quadriceps, hamstrings, core muscles.*

**8. Kick-the-Tape Kickboxing.** Take a piece of masking tape and put it on the wall at about waist level. With your left leg slightly bent and your belly button pulled in, exhale as you kick your right leg directly to the side, leading with your right hip. Your right kneecap faces forward and your upper body leans slightly to the left as you kick. Watch your right foot to see how high you kick. Repeat the move, trying to kick your right foot on or above the tape each time. Start by doing 8 kicks with each leg, and gradually work up to 12. *Targets inner and outer thighs, core muscles.*

**9. Waist Whittler.** Holding a light dumbbell in your right hand, stand with your feet shoulder-width apart, arms by your sides, palms facing in. Keeping your chest lifted and belly button pulled in, raise your left hand and put it behind your head. With your back straight, lean to the right, lowering the dumbbell down your right leg as far as you can, until you feel a stretch on the side of your waist. Don't lean forward or back with your torso. (Imagine being stuck between two panes of glass as you do the move.) Lift back up to starting position. Do this 10 times, then switch sides and repeat. *Targets abdominals (inner and outer obliques).*

**10. Single Leg Dip/Airplane Pose.**  Stand facing away from your chair. Take a giant step forward, then lift your right foot behind you and place the top of your foot on the chair seat. Keeping your torso upright and your belly button pulled in, bend both knees into a lunge, left knee directly over left ankle; simultaneously extend both arms out to the side for balance. Exhale as you straighten your legs to return to starting position. Do this 8 times. On the 8th time, before returning to starting position, lean forward so your body weight is directly over your left foot, then slowly lower your torso and lift your right foot until both your torso and left leg are parallel to the floor, simultaneously extending your arms out to the sides. Hold for up to 30 seconds, or as long as you can. Lift your torso to an upright position and lower your foot to the floor. Switch sides and repeat. *Targets buttocks, inner and outer thighs, quadriceps, hamstrings, core muscles; improves balance.*

## Cool-Down Stretches

**Knee Crossover Lift.** Lie on your back with your knees bent. Cross your left foot over your right knee and pull your right leg in toward your chest. Breathe deeply as you hold for 30 seconds, or as long as you can. Switch sides and repeat. *Stretches hip, buttocks, lower back.*

**Seated Reach.** Sit on the floor with your right leg extended and left leg bent, the sole of your left foot against your right inner thigh. Keeping your back as straight as possible, reach toward your right foot until you feel a gentle tension in your lower back and hamstrings. Breathe deeply as you hold for 30 seconds, or as long as you can. Switch sides and repeat. *Stretches hamstrings, lower back, hips.*

**Straddle Stretch.** Sit on the floor with both legs extended straight and separated in a wide V. Keeping your back straight and your hands on the floor in front of you, lean forward until you feel a gentle stretch in your inner thighs and hamstrings. Hold for 30 seconds. Next, lean to the left and reach your hands toward your left foot. Hold for 30 seconds. Now, lean to the right and reach your hands toward your right foot. Hold for 30 seconds. *Stretches inner thighs, hamstrings, hips.*

**Child's Pose.** Start in an upright kneeling position. Sit back onto your heels, then lean forward and rest your forehead on the floor, arms by your sides, palms facing up. Allow your body to relax completely as you breathe deeply in through your nose and out through your mouth. Feel your diaphragm rising and falling as air goes in and out of your body. Let your muscles sink deeper into the floor with each breath. Stay in this pose for 10 full breaths, or as long as you like. *Soothes your lower back; rejuvenates and nurtures your body.*

# Baked Apples Stuffed with Dried Fruit and Pecans

Baked apples have been a cold-weather favorite of mine for years. This updated classic includes dried fruits and pecans for added nutrients and flavor. Serve the apples hot with low-fat frozen or regular yogurt. Make a few extras and serve them with oatmeal for a hearty breakfast.

**Makes 4 apples**

4 6-ounce red apples, such as Gala or Rome Beauty
1 tablespoon fresh lemon juice
¼ cup finely chopped dried apricots
2 tablespoons dried currants
2 tablespoons chopped pecans, toasted
2 tablespoons packed dark brown sugar
¼ teaspoon cinnamon

⅛ teaspoon ground nutmeg
1 tablespoon unsalted butter (½ tablespoon softened and ½ tablespoon cut into 4 pieces)
½ cup unfiltered apple cider
¼ teaspoon vanilla
½ cup low-fat vanilla or maple yogurt

1. Preheat oven to 350°F.

2. Core apples using an apple corer. Stand apples up and make 4 evenly spaced vertical cuts starting from the top of each apple and stopping halfway from bottom. This keeps the apple intact. Brush the inside of each apple with lemon juice and stand apples in a 9-inch ceramic or glass pie plate.

3. Toss together the dried apricots, currants, pecans, brown sugar, cinnamon, and nutmeg in a bowl. With your fingers, rub softened butter into dried-fruit mixture until well combined.

4. Pack the center of each apple with the dried-fruit mixture. Put a pat of the remaining butter on top of each apple. Pour the cider and vanilla around the apples. Cover pie plate with foil.

5. Place pie plate in the middle of the oven. Bake apples, basting once, until they're just tender when pierced with a fork, about 40 minutes. Remove the foil and continue to bake another 20 to 30 minutes until the apples are very tender, but not falling apart.

6. Transfer to serving dishes and spoon sauce over and around the apples. Serve with dollops of vanilla or maple yogurt.

# CHAPTER NINE

# The Amazing Abs Bonus Workout
## . . . Starring Cindy Crawford

*T*he first time I met supermodel Cindy Crawford, she was pregnant with her first child. She came to me because she wanted to make an exercise video that would help women get back in shape after having a baby. She had heard about me through friends, and knew that I'd gained a lot of weight during my first pregnancy. (I put on a whopping eighty pounds when I was pregnant with my twins!) With so few postnatal fitness resources available, I thought the video sounded like an excellent idea and quickly signed on to help.

Cindy and I put together a three-part program to help new moms ease back into an exercise routine after pregnancy. The program featured three separate workouts that got progressively longer and more challenging to provide a "building block" approach to getting back into shape. The first two segments consisted of 12- and 14-minute workouts designed for post-pregnancy recovery. The longer, 40-minute segment was a total-body workout that included cardio, weights, and abdominal work. Our plan was to start filming the video, called *Cindy Crawford: A New Dimension*, three months after Cindy delivered her baby.

Even though Cindy is genetically blessed, she knows her body isn't going to stay that way if she doesn't work at it. I'm happy to say that she's a very committed exerciser. Aside from modeling and acting, Cindy works as a spokeswoman for a number of different companies and does charity work. She's constantly flying back and forth between her homes in New York and Los Angeles. But no matter how busy she is, she manages to

" When I was pregnant with my first baby, I developed an exercise program with Kathy for new moms. Kathy designed exercises that were easy to follow but incredibly effective. Her realistic approach to exercise is the reason why so many women have written to me about how the tape has helped them to get back into their pre-pregnancy shape. In fact, many women say that they are in better shape now than they were before they got pregnant. Kathy's workouts really give you results. The abdominal exercises are great—they get right to the spot that you want to tighten. Working out with Kathy was something I looked forward to. "

—Cindy Crawford

## Workout Sneak Preview

This five-minute ab-blasting routine targets your four primary abdominal muscles for a fast, supereffective workout. These are some of the exercises that Cindy Crawford used to regain her pre-pregnancy shape after having her first baby. By doing them three times a week, in conjunction with the other workouts in this book and a healthy diet, you can achieve a sexier, flatter, firmer midsection. Bon voyage, beach coverup!

squeeze in her workouts. She's also a very healthy eater. She always tries to make smart nutritional choices, and never goes too long without having a meal or snack, which helps keep her body energized and prevents overeating.

Cindy continued exercising throughout her pregnancy, doing a lot of walking as well as weight training. After she gave birth to her son Presley, she started doing the first workout segment from our video as soon as she felt ready and had gotten her doctor's permission. About two weeks later, she switched to the second workout; then, two weeks after that, she moved to the third. She followed our three-prong, post-pregnancy program faithfully, and by the time we shot the video, she looked amazing. She certainly didn't look like she had recently given birth.

## White Chocolate Meringue Drops

Carrie Wiatt has created a dieter's delight with these sweet treats. They're so good, it's hard to believe they're fat-free and contain only 19 calories each. Even your kids will love them!

**Makes 25 cookies**

3 whole egg whites
½ dash cream of tartar
½ cup granulated sugar

2 teaspoons vanilla extract
½ cup vanilla chips—miniature

1. Preheat oven to 250°F. Line baking sheets with parchment paper and set aside.

2. In a large bowl, beat the egg whites with cream of tartar at high speed until they form peaks. Beat in sugar one tablespoon at a time, then beat in vanilla. Reduce speed. Fold in chips with a rubber spatula.

3. Drop the mixture by leveled tablespoons onto baking sheets about 1 inch apart. Bake for 1 hour. Turn off the oven. Allow the cookies to dry in the oven for 2 hours.

Of course, not everyone is able to bounce back from childbirth so quickly. Cindy was in great shape before she got pregnant, and didn't gain too much weight while she was expecting, which certainly helped. But it also had to do with genetics. Cindy is a supermodel for a reason. She naturally has a long, slender frame, and her body responds quickly to exercise. As I mentioned earlier, it took me more than a year to fully recover from each pregnancy. While regular workouts and healthy eating habits helped me lose the excess pounds and firm up again, my body, especially my abdominals, will never be the same after having three babies. Regardless of what kind of exercise I do, I'll never again have the rippled midsection that I had in my twenties. But over time, by being persistent, I was able to shed the roll of flab around my middle and significantly improve the shape and tone of my ab muscles.

Whether or not you've had a baby, chances are you'd like your tummy to look more toned. A sexy, sculpted midsection is on the "better-body wish list" for most women. While a six-pack may not be realistic, doing exercises to strengthen your abdominal muscles can help you achieve a much flatter, firmer look. Even more important, it's essential for feeling and performing your best. Your abs are the center of your body. Everything you do, from rising out of a chair to walking to swinging a golf club, stems from your core. Keeping these middle muscles strong is crucial for good balance, beautiful posture, and a healthy, injury-proof back.

But bear in mind: Ab exercises alone may not give you the flat, sculpted appearance that you're seeking. To really look toned around your middle, some of you will need to lose some body fat. By doing so, you'll allow the underlying muscles to be more visible while improving your overall health. As I explained in Chapter 1, the best way to shed excess pounds is through a combination of cardiovascular exercise, strength training, and

Targeting your abdominals can be tricky. For best results from any midsection workout, you need to know how to fully engage your ab muscles. Visualization and deep breathing can help you make a connection between your mind and your muscles, so you can isolate and contract your abdominals more effectively. If you're doing it correctly, you should be able to feel your target muscles working the entire time. Here are three tips that can help you make the most of every exercise.

**Tap your spine.** To zero in on your abdominals, pull your belly button in, as if you were trying to touch your spine.

**Breathe deeply.** As you contract your ab muscles, exhale through your mouth to remove the air from your diaphram. When you release the muscles, take a deep breath in through your nose.

**Play the accordion.** On Moves 6 through 10, visualize your abdominal wall as an accordion stretching from your lower rib cage to your hip bones. Before starting these exercises, the accordion should be completely expanded and filled with air. As you execute them, the accordion should close completely, and all the air should be compressed out.

a healthful diet. If you're following the weekly workout program and nutritional advice in this book, you should be on your way.

If you don't get instant results, please don't be discouraged. Even if you can't visually see the changes, you can revel in the knowledge that you're doing something incredibly important for your body. If you remain committed to eating right and exercising regularly, you will notice a difference in your appearance—I promise! So be patient, and stay focused on how much better all of this exercise is making you feel. A slimmer, sleeker midriff shouldn't be far behind.

A few of the moves in this bonus ab program are from Cindy's *New Dimension* video, but they aren't only for new mothers. Coupled with the other workouts in this book, these super-effective exercises will help you strengthen and sculpt your core muscles, regardless of your age and childbearing status. They're designed to work all four major abdominal muscles, including the rectus abdominis (the visible "six-pack" muscle), the inner and outer obliques (the sides of your waist), and the transverse abdominis (a deep muscle that helps flatten your belly). What's also important is that you'll work these muscles from different angles and at different tempos, which is key to maximum results.

To get firmer and more defined, you don't need to spend twenty minutes doing ab exercises every day. This five-minute workout, performed three times a week, is all you really need. But you need to do it consistently. For fast, visible results, you also need to learn how to isolate your abdominal muscles (to find out how, refer to the Abs-olutely Perfect tip box on the opposite page). So make these moves a regular part of your exercise program, and you'll be modeling a sexier, firmer midriff before you know it!

# The Amazing Abs
# Bonus Workout

Do this bonus ab workout three times a week, with a rest day in between sessions. For example, do it on Mondays, Wednesdays, and Fridays, or on Tuesdays, Thursdays, and Saturdays. As you get stronger, you can add a fourth day, if desired.

### What You'll Need

- Towel or exercise mat
- Medium-sized ball
- 20 playing cards

## Warm-up

Standing Side Stretch.  Stand with your feet hip-width apart, knees slightly bent, chest lifted, belly button pulled in, arms by your sides. Exhale as you extend your right arm up toward the ceiling, reaching it over your head and to the left, so you feel the stretch down the right side of your body. Breathe deeply as you hold for 5 counts, then switch sides and repeat.

**Knee Lift and Kick.** Stand with your feet together, chest lifted, and belly button pulled in. Keeping your left knee slightly bent, exhale as you lift your right knee up toward your chest. Lower to starting position, then repeat with your left knee. Continue alternating sides until you have done 5 lifts with each knee. Next, bring your right knee up and extend your leg into a kick, reaching forward with left arm. Alternate sides until you've done 5 lifts and kicks with each knee.

Repeat the Standing Side Stretch, then take out your towel or exercise mat and get down on the floor for your workout.

## The Workout

**1. Forearm Plank.** *Your ultimate goal should be to hold your body in the forearm plank position for 60 seconds. If you can't do it at first, just do your best. Try to hold the position slightly longer during each workout. It may take a month or two to work up to a full minute, but that's OK. Stick with it, and you'll love the results.* Kneel on all fours, then drop onto your forearms, elbows on the floor directly under your shoulders. Walk your feet back until your legs are straight, hips lifted, so your body forms a straight line from head to heels. Keep your shoulder blades down and belly button pulled in. Don't drop your hips or let your lower back cave in. Breathe deeply as you hold this pose for as long as you can, up to 60 seconds. *Targets abdominals (rectus abdominis, inner and outer obliques, transverse abdominis), shoulders, hips, legs.*

**2. Mouse House.** *This is one of my favorite exercises. I learned it from fitness expert Kathy Smith. She calls it a mouse house, which is exactly how you need to picture it.* Lie facedown on the floor with your arms crossed and your head resting on your forearms. Keeping your buttocks relaxed and pelvis stable, exhale as you pull your belly button in and up off the floor. Visualize that there's enough space for a mouse between your belly and the floor, but don't let him out! Do this 10 times. *Targets abdominals (transverse abdominis).*

**3. Plank Knee Pull-In.** Start in a straight-leg push-up or plank position, with your hands in line with your shoulders, hips lifted, legs extended behind you, body weight resting on your toes. Pull your belly button in toward your spine. Maintaining this position, exhale as you bring your right knee in toward your chest. Hold while gently lowering your chin toward the knee. Return to starting position, then repeat with left knee. Continue alternating legs until you have done 10 on each side. *Targets abdominals (rectus abdominis), back, chest, shoulders.*

**4. Bicycle.** Lie on your back with your knees bent, lower back pressed into the floor. Rest your hands behind your head. Keeping your belly button pulled in, exhale as you extend your right leg out straight; simultaneously lift your shoulders off the floor and bring your right elbow and left knee toward each other. Inhale, then exhale as you repeat the exercise, using the opposite arm and leg. Keep the movement slow and controlled, and focus on using your abdominal muscles, not your legs or shoulders, to do the work. Continue alternating sides until you have done 10 on each side. Rest for 30 seconds, then repeat. *Targets abdominals (rectus abdominis, inner and outer obliques).*

**5. Reverse Crunch.** Lie on your back with your arms by your sides, palms facing down. Extend both legs straight up in the air. Exhale as you use your abdominal muscles to lift your hips about an inch off the floor. Inhale as you lower your hips to starting position. Keep your legs as straight as you can; don't swing or kick them. Don't cheat by pushing with your hands. Do 3 sets of 8. As you get stronger, try keeping your hips lifted up off the floor for a count or two before lowering. *Targets abdominals (lower fibers of rectus abdominis).*

**6. Card Sit-up.** Hold 15 playing cards in your right hand. Lie on your back with your knees bent, arms extended above your head. Exhale as you use your ab muscles to lift your torso up into a seated position, simultaneously using your left hand to deal a card onto the floor in between your legs. Lower to starting position, then repeat until all cards are dealt. Next, continue the sit-ups, picking up one card at a time until all cards are back in your right hand. *Targets abdominals (rectus abdominis).*

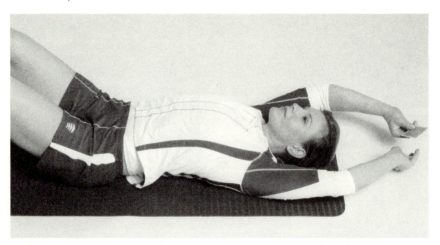

**7. Straight-Leg Crunch with Ball.** Lie on your back with your legs extended straight up in the air. Hold a medium-sized ball between your knees. Place your hands loosely behind your head. Exhale as you use your ab muscles to slowly lift your head and shoulder blades up off the floor. Keep your chin off your chest and look up toward your feet. Do this 15 times. Rest for 15 to 30 seconds, then repeat. *Targets abdominals (rectus abdominis).*

**8. Knee Slide.** Lie on your back with your knees bent, your left hand behind your head, and your right hand resting on your right thigh. Exhale as you lift your shoulder blades up off the floor, and slide your right hand up to your right knee. Keep your right arm straight and your right hand firmly against your thigh. When you push against your thigh, your abs are forced to work harder to lift your upper body higher. Do 2 sets of 15 on each side. *Targets abdominals (upper fibers of rectus abdominis).*

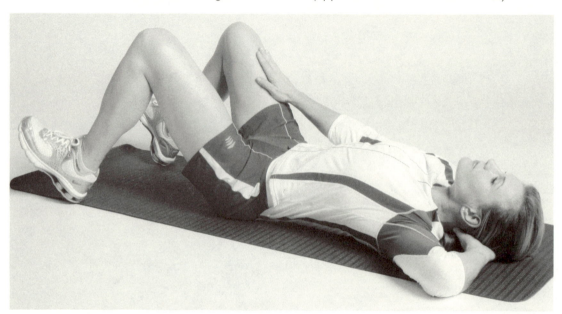

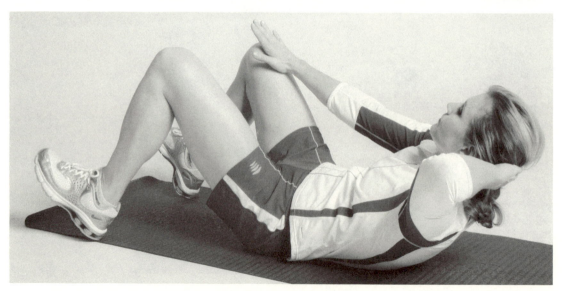

**9. Oblique Card Sit-up.** Hold 20 playing cards in your left hand. Lie on your back with your knees bent, arms above your head. Exhale as you use your ab muscles to lift your upper torso into a seated position, simultaneously using your right hand to deal a card onto the floor next to the outside of your left foot. As you reach across to place the card on the floor, you should feel the muscles on the left side of your abdomen engage. Lower to starting position, then repeat until you've dealt 10 cards. Now switch hands, so the 10 remaining cards are in your left hand, and continue the exercise until you've dealt the remaining cards onto the floor next to the outside of your right foot. When all the cards have been dealt, repeat the exercise, picking up the cards by your left foot, one at a time. Switch hands and pick up the cards by your right foot, one at a time. *Targets abdominals (inner and outer obliques).*

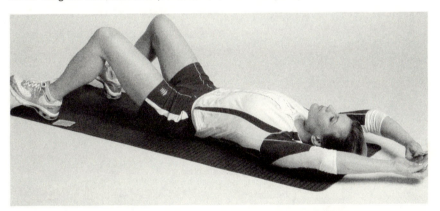

**10. 4-Count Combo.** *This exercise is to a 4-count cadence. It works well if you count it out loud.* Lie on your back with your knees bent and above your hips, hands resting behind your head, chin off your chest. Count 1: Exhale as you lift your shoulder blades straight up off the floor. Count 2: Continue to exhale as you reach your left elbow to your right knee for an oblique crunch. Count 3: Keep exhaling as you return to center (as in Count 1) for another crunch. Count 4: Inhale and lower your shoulders to starting position. Do this 8 times; then another 8 times, reaching your right elbow to your left knee on Count 2. *Targets abdominals (rectus abdominis, inner and outer obliques).*

## Cool-Down Stretches

Knee Drop. Lie on your back with your knees bent, feet together and flat on the floor, hands clasped behind your head. Lower both knees to your left side, keeping as much of your back and hips on the floor as possible. Breathe deeply as you hold for at least 30 seconds. Return to starting position, then repeat, lowering knees to your right side. *Targets core muscles (abs and lower back).*

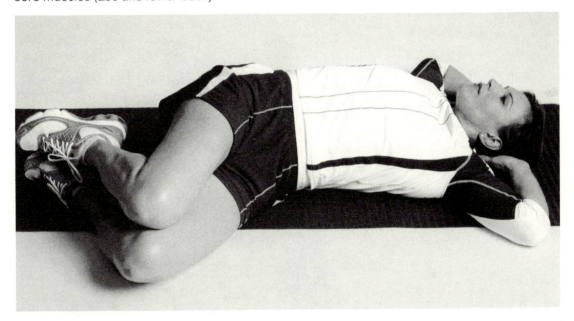

**Seated Twist.** Sit on the floor with your legs extended in front of you. Bend your left knee and place your left foot on the floor near the outside of your right knee. Place your left hand on the floor behind you for support. Keeping your buttocks planted on the floor, reach across your left knee with your right arm and turn your upper body to the left, focusing your gaze over your left shoulder. Breathe deeply as you hold for at least 30 seconds. Switch sides and repeat. *Targets core muscles.*

**Modified Cobra.** Lie facedown on the floor propped up on your elbows, elbows in line with your shoulders, fingers pointing directly forward. Exhale as you lift your head, shoulders, and chest off the floor, keeping your spine long and pressing the tops of your thighs and feet into the floor. Breathe deeply as you hold for at least 30 seconds. *Targets abdominals, chest, shoulders, neck.*

# Fruit Salad Parfait

Hollis Wilder's fresh fruit parfaits can be served as an elegant dessert for guests, or a healthy grab-and-go snack for your family. Fill either large wine glasses or small plastic cups with single servings of the parfaits. Serve immediately, or cover tightly and keep refrigerated for up to three days.

**Makes 4 servings**

**Creamy peach sauce**

1 banana
2 peaches
½ cup orange or apple juice

**Cashew cream**

½ cup raw cashews
1½ cup water
2 teaspoons maple syrup
2 cups cantaloupe balls

2 cups honeydew balls
1 cup fresh raspberries or strawberries
1 cup fresh blueberries
1 papaya, peeled, seeded, and cubed
1 mango, peeled and cubed
½ cup currants, soaked until plump (optional)
¼ cup shredded coconut
4 mint leaves

**For the peach sauce:** Put the banana, peaches, and orange or apple juice in a blender and blend until smooth.

**For the cashew cream:** Combine cashews, water, and maple syrup in a blender. Blend on high for 3 minutes, or until you have a smooth cream.

1. Place the melon balls, berries, papaya, and mango in layers in large wine glasses, alternating colors. Sprinkle each layer with the currants and coconut.

2. Spoon the peach sauce and some cashew cream over the fruit and allow them to drizzle down the layers. Top with remaining cashew cream and a mint leaf.

**Extended Child's Pose.** Start in an upright kneeling position. Sit back onto your heels, then lean forward and rest your forehead on the floor, arms extended straight in front of you. Allow your body to relax completely as you breathe deeply in through your nose and out through your mouth. Feel your diaphragm rising and falling as air goes in and out of your body. Let your muscles sink deeper into the floor with each breath. Stay in this pose for 10 full breaths, or as long as you like. *Soothes your lower back; rejuvenates and nurtures your body.*

# CHAPTER TEN

# After the Camera Stops Rolling:
## Sticking with It

*I want to thank you again for picking up this* book! I hope you've enjoyed reading about some of my personal and professional journeys, and the inspiring success stories of some of the incredible women that I train. I'm so happy you've made the decision to start taking better care of yourself and lead a healthier, more active life.

I hope that I've inspired you to get moving and eat well. I hope this program can help you get started. And I say "started" because this is just the first step. Regular exercise and healthy eating can help you improve the quality of your life and feel happier and more fulfilled—but *only* if you stick with it. What I've given you is a solid foundation that you can build on. This book contains simple exercises and practical tips that you can keep for the rest of your life, like pearls in your pocket. Whenever you need some encouragement, a quick refresher, or a bit of advice, you can open the book and pull out another pearl. As your trainer, my goal is to give you all the information and advice you need in order to change your body and your lifestyle forever. Now it's up to you to do what it takes to turn fitness into a lifelong habit.

Don't forget, one of the reasons my celebrity clients always look so fabulous is because they're consistent with their workouts. The beautifully sculpted stars featured in this book don't begin exercising six weeks before production on a movie starts, then quit immediately after the director says, "It's a wrap!" They've learned to maintain their fitness programs whether or not they're in front of the camera, so they're not calling me at the last minute looking for a miracle.

By picking up this book, you've shown that you're motivated to make a change. But long-term success requires more than just the will to start. You need the ability to start over and over again. Every day, I am challenged by my kids, my work, my home, and my lifestyle. We all have many things on our plates. Some days just don't turn out as planned! From supermodels to supermoms, we all have time constraints and obstacles. So you need to be prepared for those inevitable hurdles.

If you miss a few workouts because you're sick or swamped with work, don't give up and quit! It isn't the end of the world. Instead, toss that day or week out the window, and resolve to get back on the healthy lifestyle wagon as soon as you can. Don't forget, no matter how long it's been since your last workout, it's never too late to lace up your sneakers and get moving again.

Remember: If you fail to plan, you plan to fail. So at the beginning of each week, take out your day planner and reserve a time slot for every workout. Write them down on your calendar, just like a doctor's appointment or a parent-teacher meeting. By putting these "fitness dates" in ink, you'll be more likely to treat them as important events that can't be missed. Scheduling your workouts at the same time every day will also help you get into a routine.

If you still have trouble keeping these dates, sit down and figure out what's hindering you. If lack of time is your biggest issue, analyze your weekly schedule to determine where your time is going. Once you know your main obstacles, you can find ways to work around them. You may also notice activities, such as watching TV or blow-drying your hair, that aren't as important as exercise, in which case you can vow to start using that time more productively.

Talk to your family, friends, and coworkers about your need for exercise, and ask for their support. Studies show that people with high levels of social support tend to have more success maintaining a regular fitness program—so it's key to get your loved ones on board. If you're missing your workouts because you're overloaded with work projects or household chores, you must learn to delegate, accept help from others, and just say "No."

Research also suggests that keeping a written record of your workouts can help you stay on track. So in a journal or a notebook, log in the date, duration, and details (what you did and how it made you feel) of each exercise session. At the end of each month, look back to see what you've achieved. If you've met your goals, reward yourself with a healthy treat, such as a massage, a new workout outfit, or an extra hour of sleep. You're changing your life for the better, and you should be proud of yourself!

To keep your workouts stimulating and fresh, you should continue mixing it up in the months ahead. If you do the same exercises all the time, your muscles will adapt, and you'll eventually hit a fitness plateau. To get past the plateau, you'll need to push your body a little harder or challenge your muscles with something new. For your strength workouts, try using heavier dumbbells, doing more repetitions, or incorporating new exercises into your routine. For cardio, you can go a little faster, a little farther, or add some hills. Or switch to a new activity such as cycling, in-line skating, or a trendy cardio class at your local gym.

Setting goals is another great way to stay motivated and focused on the positive changes that you're making. Try to come up with new challenges for yourself in addition to the suggestions in the workouts here. For example, you might decide to train for a walking event, a bike trip, or a 10-kilometer race. Or you might decide to make this year's family vacation a camping trip to a national park, where day hikes, biking, or kayaking will be a major part of the activities.

Studies show that most people need to stick with their exercise plan for approximately thirty to sixty days before their commitment truly takes hold. So be as consistent as humanly possible in the next few months. If you need more ideas to help keep you motivated, you can subscribe to receive my daily Health-E-tips via e-mail (go to www.healthetips.com for details).

The women in my Hidden Hills classes tell me how much they appreciate my guidance. But for me, it's the other way around. I appreciate them more than they will ever know. And the same goes for you, too. *You* are the ones who motivate me to continue finding fun new ways to get a cardio workout, target those problem spots, and stay active. So thank you again!

Remember that you only have one body. You can't trade it in for a new one. So treat it right! There's nothing more attractive than a woman who is healthy and strong, and who can stand firmly on her own two feet. A balanced menu of exercise and good food is the fountain of youth. So get out there, have fun, and be healthy!

Stay fit,
Sincerely,

# Acknowledgments

Writing a book takes many people. People who have given so much time and commitment to this book. To begin, Stacy Whitman. I would not have had a book without you. You have put my ideas and philosophies into words that will help people improve the quality of their lives. And your sister, Wynne Whitman. I didn't get to meet you, Wynne, but I owe you a thank you for all your work on this book. My agent, Matthew Guma, I wouldn't have a book without you, period. Your passion and inspiration are truly amazing, and I can only be grateful that you are in my life.

To my editor, Ann Campbell—words cannot express my gratitude for your dedication to this book. Also, Sharon House, you don't know how grateful I am to have you watching out for me. Your tradional sensibility, your gracious personality, and you perseverance in getting me where I am today are remarkable. I couldn't do it without you—thank you.

A book like this one cannot stand on the shelf with words alone. The photography is the element that makes it come alive. Without Eric Asla, the book would have no life. Eric, your eye is incredible. You are a lovely person; your sensitivity and warmth enabled me to be me in front of the lens. I cannot thank you enough.

Many thanks to those who made the shooting days memorable: Debbie F., Kathy H., and Helen J. Above all, I thank my family. My best friend, partner, and lifelong soulmate, Billy. I love you, and thank you for putting up with me during this whole process. And every day, I get to realize why we are here: my children. Their loving faces bring happiness to me morning, noon, and night. Each day brings us another experience here on earth. Take time for yourselves and don't miss it.

## Photo Permissions

Diligent efforts have been made to locate the copyright owners of all the photographs contained in this book, but some have not been located. In the event a photograph has been used without permission, the copyright owner should contact the author, c/o Broadway Books, 1745 Broadway, New York, NY 10019, Attn: Editorial.

Title page: (*clockwise from top left*) Courtesy of Kathy Kaehler, NBC/Getty Images, Danny Moder, Frank Trapper/Corbis Sygma

Page xvi: Tracy Mochel Photography

Page 38: Steve Granitz/WireImages.com

Page 42: Courtesy of Kathy Kaehler

Page 62: Courtesy of Kathy Kaehler

Page 67: Eric Asla

Page 68: Courtesy of Kathy Kaehler

Page 88: NBC/Getty Images

Page 91: NBC/Getty Images

Page 116: Courtesy of Kathy Kaehler

Page 148: Frank Trapper/Corbis

Page 153: Danny Moder

Page 157: Danny Moder

Page 178: Mark Seliger/Corbis Outline

Page 202: Frank Trapper/Corbis Sygma

Page 204: Mike Russ Photography

Page 205: Courtesy of GoodTimes Entertainment

# WORKOUT AT HOME
## — with —
# KATHY KAEHLER *basics* DVDs

## total **fitness** workout

- 5 minutes a day toward total body conditioning.
- Work all three sides of The Fitness Triangle: Cardio, Strength, and Flexibility.
- Increase lean muscle mass, improve balance and posture.
- Complete the entire 35-minute routine or choose a 5-minute conditioning segment each day.
- The same "back to basic" techniques that have toned and shaped your favorite stars!

## workout **class**

- Classic moves on the step and on the floor.
- 8-minute warm up, heart pumping half-hour of step cardio, 10-minute tone and stretch cool down.
- Increase endurance, reshape your entire body, burn calories, have fun!
- For those who are new to step or looking for an effective alternative to regular gym classes.
- Can be done entirely on the floor for an effective cardio workout.

**Plus: Each DVD contains Health-E-Tips™: Kaehler's personal tips for living a healthy and well-balanced lifestyle.**